NO MORE HURTING

This wonderful book reached deep into my brokeness, revealing issues that I previously didn't have a name for or wasn't willing to confront. It has brought about major healing and my future now feels like it has purpose and meaning; things I never thought I would have. I shed many a tear during the course of this book, but I couldn't put it down. Hope has been restored!

Jayne

My grandparents were missionaries in China in the 40's and 50's and helped bring an end to the custom of binding the feet of baby girls. As my grandmother unbound the feet of wee girls in China, setting them free to live and move without physical pain, I see the ministry of Gwen and Sandy Purdie as God's agent of healing and release to minds and spirits bound and wounded by sexual abuse. This book will be the key to the release of many people so they are able to live in freedom and dance with joy once again.

Kathryn, S.U. Scotland

No more Hurting *has been a tremendous resource coming out Gwen Purdie's lifetime experience of helping people in this area. Her approach is wise, practical and full of godly insight!*

Written by someone who helps abused people

Gwen shares a lifetime of experience and a depth of spiritual insight as she delves into the disturbing world of sexual abuse. When reading this book one realises that God cares deeply for the abused.

Stephen McQuoid, Principal, Tilsley College, Motherwell

NO MORE HURTING

LIFE BEYOND
SEXUAL ABUSE

GWEN PURDIE

© Gwen Purdie 2004

ISBN 978-1-85792-679-8

Published in 2004
Reprinted 2009
by
Christian Focus Publications Ltd,
Geanies House, Fearn, Tain, Ross-shire,
IV20 1TW, Scotland

www.christianfocus.com

Cover design by Alister MacInnes

Printed by Norhaven A/S, Denmark

CONTENTS

'O afflicted city,
lashed by storms and not comforted,
I will build you with stones of turquoise,
your foundations with sapphires.
I will make your battlements of rubies,
your gates of sparkling jewels,
and all your walls of precious stones'
Isaiah 54:11-12 (NIV).

FOREWORD

Through many years of counselling and praying with the most severely abused, Gwen McDowell Purdie has journeyed deep into the heart of God's love for the broken-hearted. She knows well not only our Lord's power to heal, but His yearning to 'give them a beautiful headdress instead of ashes, the oil of gladness instead of mourning, the garment of praise instead of a faint spirit' [see Isa 61: 1-4 ESV]. To say it yet another way, she knows that our Lord delights in opening the prison doors of sexual abuse and calling forth His little ones into freedom.

To work alongside Gwen is to see why she succeeded so remarkably as a counsellor and a pioneer in training others in counselling. She has a unique capacity to first listen attentively as a person bares his grief and tells his story, and then to confidently lead the hurting one into the healing Presence of God. She knows how to ask the right questions - those that get to the very heart of the matter, no matter how painful. She possesses an uncanny Scot's commonsense and cannot easily be fooled; she will always settle for nothing less than the full truth. Yet, she possesses an extraordinary wit that ministers the medicine of good cheer and hope to weary souls.

We give thanks that *No More Hurting: Life Beyond Sexual Abuse* is now available to the people of Scotland, a folk she and her husband, Sandy, have so well served. We trust that those who desperately need the guidance and encouragement she holds out will be led unerringly to it.

Leanne Payne
President, Pastoral Care Ministries, Inc.

ABOUT THE AUTHOR

Gwen Purdie (nee McDowell) was born and raised in Scotland. Becoming a Christian changed her life dramatically and led her into professional social work, desiring to see people made whole. After ten years as a specialist with adolescents and alcoholics, Gwen moved on to pioneer a work in Christian counselling in her homeland. Gwen was founder and director of Dove Christian Counselling, which still operates today. She has been working with emotional needs in people for thirty eight years. In 1996 Gwen married Sandy Purdie and they have been working together since then, making every effort to help people towards wholeness. Gwen has a particular heart for reaching abused people with hope. Sandy and Gwen continue to see individuals and couples as Christian consultants with a healing ministry that offers careful listening to a person or a couple along with Christian healing prayer if the person so chooses. This consultancy allows them to work in mediation, training and lecturing in churches and in other organisations.

Gwen and Sandy now live and minister on the Isle of Bute and in Edinburgh, allowing them to offer a service in both the east and west of Scotland. They are members of Bellevue Chapel, Edinburgh and also attend Rothesay Christian Fellowship when on the island.

www.lethem-lodge.co.uk

PREFACE

Over the years I have met many hurting people, who will probably never find their way to a counsellor nor be able to share their pain with anyone who might help them. It is with them in mind that I have written this book, in the hope that they will be encouraged to grasp the fact that there can be life beyond sexual abuse and beyond all the implications and symptoms that so often accompany such an experience. It is also my hope that it will be useful to others who may be trying to understand the pain involved in sexual abuse and its consequences.

If someone has been sexually abused, he or she may find reading this book disturbing. Facing abuse and the emotions which go with it can be an overwhelming experience, but recovery from abuse usually occurs in small, steady steps. Reading this book could be very helpful. Subjects may be raised in the course of this book that the reader does not yet feel ready to face. There is a right time to face issues, and that timing is unique to every individual. Care should be taken to stay safe. It is wise to follow intuitive feelings which may rise to the surface. This book can be laid down and returned to at a later date, and that may be the wise thing to do if the reader feels unready to cope with the issues it is highlighting in his (or her) life.

This book is unashamedly written from a Christian perspective, but this should not detract from its ability to help anyone who wants to recover from the effects of sexual abuse. Practical suggestions and sources of further help (in the form of either books, websites or telephone helplines) are scattered throughout the book, in the hope that some readers will be able to move forward in their journey towards healing.

Many people have helped me in the course of writing this book. A very deep debt of gratitude goes to those who have allowed me to share something of their experiences. All of these people appear under assumed names in this book to protect their identities.

I am also deeply grateful to:

- Many people who have contributed 'silently' to this book by sharing their stories and their hearts over the years. It must be evident that I owe a large debt to many abused people – I thank God for each of you. You have been my greatest teachers.
- The friend who typed the initial manuscript from hand–written notes.
- Jane Ferris for exceptional editorial help which was provided by Christian Focus Publications. Any remaining errors are my sole responsibility.
- Bruntsfield Evangelical Church, Edinburgh, my church for twenty–six years, for having the foresight to support me as a Christian counsellor. As a result, hundreds of abused people have been helped over the years.
- The large army of people who have prayed this book into being.
- My colleagues at Dove Christian Counselling. We walked and talked together; we cried and laughed together, and this book is a product of these precious years.

- My wonderful husband, Sandy, who supported me with endless enthusiasm.

Special thanks must go to the following for their support, encouragement and help in countless ways before and during the writing of this book: Houston and Jenny A, Vikki B, Kathy D, Pamela E, Findlay H, Jane F, David G, Allister J, Ruth J, Anne L, Ruth M, Douglas and Liz Mc, George McK, Leanne P, Elizabeth R, Grace R, Cathie W, Fiona W and many others.

CHAPTER 1

TRUTH SUBMERGED

> I never dared tell anyone what I thought might have happened in my childhood. In my family I would have got a beating. I would never have been believed and it would have all been my fault anyway. I guess I didn't believe it myself, or at least, I didn't want to believe it. However, it is now obvious that I have all the emotional scars that match having been sexually abused. I struggle big–time to relate to people and I am just waiting for something else to go wrong in my life.

There are so many people today hurting because of sexual abuse. In the course of this book two people, whom I call Heather and Henry, share something of their journey towards healing from the effects of sexual abuse. Henry is a well-qualified and experienced person who works in a professional capacity. Heather is an interesting lady who until her later years had no memory of having been abused. Their stories tell how, in different ways, they were both abused, and some of the steps they have been through in order to find healing. Others have agreed to share incidents from their experience, and also appear under assumed names and identities. This has allowed them to share facts about their abuse and recovery without implicating other people. It may be that readers will be able to identify with some of these experiences, in which case I trust that their stories will give encouragement and offer hope that there really can be healing.

Facts and figures

Many people find it difficult to accept that sexual abuse is anything more than a relatively unusual phenomenon in our society. So when a high-profile case of sexual abuse hits the headlines, particularly when children are involved, there is a public outcry, and it is the exceptional and extraordinary nature of the offence that is emphasised. Most people, I imagine, would prefer not to acknowledge how common sexual abuse is, especially within families. It is far more comfortable to submerge this kind of knowledge under horrified outrage at the rare and exceptional incident. Tragically, however, sexual abuse is all too common in our society, although it is usually submerged beneath a surface of apparent normality, kept secret behind the closed doors of respectability. The reality is that sexual abuse is happening today, and many people are struggling to emerge from the pain and torn emotions that come from that abuse.

Sexual abuse in Britain is difficult to measure. Since it is thought that up to 80% of sexual assaults against children go unreported, official statistics are bound to fall far short of the real figures.[1] This suggests that figures we have are only the tip of the iceberg, but the following statistics give some idea as to how widespread the problem is. The Child Protection

---

1. *Myths and facts about child sexual abuse.* Rape Crisis Federation Wales and England, Unit 7, Provident Works, Newdigate Street, Nottingham, NG7 4FD. www.rapecrisis.co.uk.

Registers for 2002 indicate that there were 2,800 children in England, 231 children in Northern Ireland, 253 children in Wales and 249 children in Scotland on these registers because they were identified as having been sexually abused. The recognised definition of child sexual abuse for the purposes of these registers is the use of an under sixteen-year-old child for an adult's sexual pleasure.[2] A Home Office report in 1998, commenting on the recorded offences of sexual abuse against children, said:

> In terms of official statistics, the indecent assault of females under 16 is by far the most common offence involving children. In these cases an offender is formally dealt with: in 1995 this offence resulted in 2,116 cautions or convictions, representing about 50% of all sexual offences recorded against children.[3]

These were, of course, just the legally proved cases. A report by the Rape Crisis Federation in 2001 observed:

> ... child sexual abuse occurs within all areas of society and throughout the world. Children of all ages, races, religions and classes are abused. Children with a disability are particularly vulnerable – being nearly five times more likely to be abused than able-bodied children. 90% of disabled women are raped abused or assaulted at some time in their lives ... With 90% of their abusers being known to them.[4] It is also true that the person who is abused knows the abuser in most cases of actual rape.[5]

---

2. Source material: The NSPCC Library and Information Service.
3. Police Research Series Paper 99, Sex offending against children: Understanding the risk, Don Grubin.
4. Margaret Kennedy, keynote address, Violence, Abuse and Women's Citizenship Conference, 10th November 1996.
5. The Scottish Rape Crisis Network provides help and support for victims of rape. They are contactable at PO Box 53, Glasgow, Scotland, G2 1YR, Tel. 0141 552 3200. For international contact details see appendix.

Although estimates vary, most studies show that between 1 in 10 and 1 in 4 children will have experienced sexual abuse before they reach adulthood. Although women do sometimes abuse children, the overwhelming majority of abusers (some reports suggest up to 95%) are male and heterosexual.[6] These statistics support my opinion, based on many years of counselling experience, that sexual abuse is horrifyingly common, frequently unreported or disbelieved, and is something that society at large has yet to begin to face up to.

From its inception twenty years ago, our Christian counselling practice was general in nature, and we never advertised our service. In all those years of working in counselling we were never short of clients, and for the most part ran with a sizable waiting list. Right from the start some of our clients needed help because they had been abused. In any given year there were always a significant number of clients seeking help because of sexual abuse and the resulting symptoms, and 50% of all the clients we saw, both men and women, had issues with abuse. With the passing of the years, more people, and especially more men, have come specifically as a result of experiencing abuse. I am of the view that it has become more socially acceptable to talk of past abuse, and men are probably also more aware that abuse is not something that only happens to women. It would also be true to say that there is far more coverage in the media nowadays of sexual abuse. There has also been more awareness in recent years that counselling help is available. Generally, more men are coming for counselling than previously, whether or not they have been abused. During the last four years, of the clients who presented for counselling, 51% of the women and 10% of the men reported that they had been sexually abused. Of those who were abused, 30% of

6. Milton Keynes Rape Crisis, Rape Crisis Federation Wales and England, see page 14, footnote 1.

women and 29% of men were abused before the age of sixteen. In the same period 4% of those we counselled were perpetrators of sexual abuse, two of whom had abused children.

The unpalatable truth is that sexual abuse happens and is damaging and destructive. Every abusive incident, however seemingly trivial, is deeply concerning. Any sexual abuse has the potential to devastate the person affected. It is not necessarily any less damaging to be shown pornographic pictures than to be raped. Neither is good because of the damage it can do inside a person. Sexual abuse adversely affects people's thought life, their decisions and choices, and their feelings. It also affects their perceptions of their body, and has relational and social implications. As a result of sexual abuse a person may not be able to enjoy sexual experience in marriage, or may seek comfort through substance abuse or indiscriminate sexual contacts. Relationships can be difficult, especially trusting people and forming new friendships. Past hurts can stand in the way of progress, and there can be anger, depression, lack of confidence and well-being, guilt, self-blame and self-hate.

I remember a client who came for help a long time ago. She thought she was 'going off her head', because after being happily married for some years, she suddenly and unexpectedly recalled a childhood experience of sexual abuse. The way it affected her was to make her experience inordinate anger towards her husband, who had done nothing to deserve this anger. Trying to manage her anger brought her to crisis point. Through counselling she began to see that it was really her abuser she was angry with and that she would need to work through the roots of her emotions. This lady and her husband were able to resume a normal relationship once the childhood issues had been sorted out.

Anyone who has experienced abuse, especially if they were abused as a child, needs reassurance that they are not, or need not be, permanently maimed emotionally, and that many of their efforts to cope and put the past behind them can make them strong and capable individuals.[7]

Who are the sexually abused?

Most of my counselling practice has taken place in Scotland, although many of my clients had originally lived in other parts of Britain or overseas. Sexual abuse can happen anywhere and to anyone, regardless of gender or age: to boys and girls, men and women, rich and poor, of any or no religious belief. In my experience, far more women seek counselling help than men, and it does seem that more women than men are abused. However, men do not suffer any less than women from the consequences that come from having been sexually abused. To have suffered from sexual abuse as a child or as an adult is a very traumatic experience, but it needs to be made clear that it is never the abused person's fault that they have been the subject of abuse. The abuser is solely responsible for the abuse.

At an everyday level, the sexually abused are not identifiable. They are hidden behind all sorts of circumstances, situations and appearances. The beautiful young lady in the workplace might as easily have been abused as the homemaker or the young man who serves in the local bank. I have counselled people from all walks of life who have been sexually abused. I think of the disabled lady who struggled to believe that a male relative had raped her one night. She had no strength to stop him. Then there was the university student who began to recall that her neighbour had blackmailed her as a child with sweets, as a route to abusing her. Her parents had no idea that this was happening. Then there was the housewife who became very scared of her husband and his sexual violence. A man who

7. See more in chapter 2.

came from another culture shared that his childhood was full of abuses, which he was only just able to face. The abused person is not easily recognised, but they are in our cafes, our trains, our churches and our neighbourhoods.

What can be done?
Anyone reading this book whilst still locked into an abusive situation should try somehow to get help to get out of that situation. Becoming free may be difficult to imagine and bring to pass, but full recovery and freedom is possible. Ongoing abuse stunts a person's growth and feeds continuing fear and trauma. It is unhealthy to stay in an abusive situation, but there may seem no option. Over many years, I have supported a number of adults who have found themselves powerless to leave. God alone knows the deep heartache involved. I believe, however, from my observation of many people who have been suffering, that to be able to fully embrace life after abuse, the abuse has to stop.

The first step is to confide in someone who is to be trusted, a doctor, minister, social worker, specialist, counsellor or a good friend. Intervention, help, support, friendship and information are all necessary in moving towards being freed from ongoing abuse.[8]

In the case of a child, the abuse must not be allowed to continue. The appropriate authorities must be involved immediately for the child to be protected, and to enable the best provision to be made for the child's welfare. In Scotland there is a Children's Panel system designed especially with children in mind. This means that discussions are held in a less formal room than a courtroom. The Children's Panel has experience of deciding what is best for a child and his or her family. If

---

8. See more in chapter 4.

there is any concern that a child is being sexually abused, initial contact can be made with the school, the local doctor, the police (Emergency 999), social services, a counselling agency or child helplines, such as:

NSPCC National Society for the Prevention of Cruelty to Children, Child Protection Helpline, PO Box 18222, London, EC2A 3RU. Tel. 0808 800 5000, www.nspcc.org. uk email: help@nspcc.org.uk.

Children 1st (formerly the Royal Society for the Prevention of Cruelty to Children) can be found at 83 Whitehouse Loan, Edinburgh, Scotland, EH9 1AT, Tel. 0131 446 2300, www.children1st.org.uk.

Parentline Scotland can be reached through the Children 1st website or phone 0808 800 2222.[9]

Each agency has the experience and procedures to act appropriately in liaison with others. Child protection policies are in place in many agencies, including most churches.

If you are a child who is struggling in an abusive situation at the time of reading this book, please go and ask for help at school, from your doctor or at home. Certainly you should speak to a grown–up person who you feel able to trust. It is absolutely right to tell someone you are feeling upset. You can call Childline on 0800 1111. It is a free telephone service that operates twenty four hours a day and is designed to help any child or young person who is in trouble or danger. Childline states: 'Childline is confidential – which means we won't tell anyone about your call unless you want Childline to talk to somebody for you, or you are in danger.' They say if the line is busy you are to keep trying and you will get through to someone who will be able to help you.

---

9. For international contact details see the appendix.

Who abuses?

Evidence shows that abusers come from all social backgrounds, any and every type of employment and nationality, and can be of any age. From my own work with people who have been abused within their families, these families come from every economic, cultural, educational, religious and geographical background. Researchers strongly indicate that abusers are often men who are married with children, have respectable jobs and may be regular churchgoers. Some people think that Christians are exempt from abusing and would never do such a thing. Sadly, that is just not the case. Incestuous fathers can be found in caring professions and even in churches; they may speak out loudly against abuse yet be abusers themselves. It is common for offenders to strongly deny their abusive behaviour, to refuse to see their actions as a problem, and to rationalise their behaviour or place blame on something or someone else.

What is sexual abuse?

Sexual abuse, defined as any type of sexual assault upon a child or an adult, can be a one-off or a repeated event. Child sexual abuse is the sexual exploitation of a child under the age of sixteen. Sadly, both girls and boys can suffer sexual abuse from a very young age. It is the experience of being overwhelmed by an abuser's power and will which makes sexual abuse so damaging in a person's life.[10] The sexual abuse of any individual can cover a wide range of behaviours, but most often involves:

- a violation of the abused person's body, especially his or her private parts;
- a violation of will which removes a person's freedom of choice;
- a violation of privacy and personal space, giving the person a sense of powerlessness.

---

10. See more in chapter 7.

In trying to face up to past experiences, people sometimes question whether behaviour they experienced was really abusive. Those trying to help people who have been abused may have similar concerns. Understanding exactly what does and does not constitute abuse is therefore very important. The following list is one that I often use and has proved quite helpful.

Questions to ask are whether any of the following happened:

- Shown pornographic material, magazines, videos?
- Forced to listen to sex talk?
- Forced to expose sexual organs?
- Bathed in a way that caused feelings of unease?
- Made to pose for sexual photographs?
- Made to have oral sex?
- Made to look at other people's genitalia?
- Touched on the breasts or genitalia?
- Cuddled or kissed in a way that left them feeling distressed or disturbed?
- Penetrated by finger, penis or object inside the vagina or anus?
- Penetrated using force or violence?
- Raped?

It is clear from the above list that a whole variety of activities come under the label of sexual abuse. There may also be less obvious things that are abusive. You will see from the list that rape is included, but it should be noted that a person can be sexually assaulted or abused without being raped.

It is just as important to know what does not constitute abusive behaviour, particularly for those who lack an understanding of the normal expressions of affection in a family setting. For instance, it is normal and natural for children to touch their own bodies, and those of other children, in a way that makes them feel good. This is part of learning and exploring, and children should not be made to feel guilty about it. Sex play amongst children is not usually abusive, nor are normal family expressions of affection; sexual abuse does not include the kisses and cuddles and good touches that adults and children give each other. These are healthy ways in which we can express affection, reassurance and care. It is very sad that touch, such as hugging and kissing, has become such an issue in our society, and that what was once understood to be normal, healthy behaviour is now not practised to the same extent even within families for fear of accusations of abuse. This is also true in schools, where teachers dare not touch students. I know of a teacher who felt unable to comfort a five-year-old child in her class because it was against the standards laid down for the school.

Henry and Heather's stories illustrate just how damaging sexual abuse can be, and how children in particular can be left confused as to what has happened to them.

Heather was not raped, but has much to say about the symptoms of sexual abuse that she has suffered in every area of her life.

I can't imagine what being raped must feel like, but the devastation of what happened to me was bad enough. My daddy, in a way that felt like an infringement, touched me on my genitals. My response came much later because the memory of the event went deep within myself. There was a blank in my mind for years and I always knew that I feared my daddy but didn't know why. I felt I was like a pressure cooker inside. Once I realised what had happened to me, I felt violated and outraged. It seemed that the worst had happened to me. It left me with little confidence in relating and low self-esteem. It was a struggle to believe that I could ever get beyond all the accumulated pain I felt. Most people in my life to this day do not know that I have been abused. I am seen as a successful person with a stable home life. I go to church and have lots of interests in my life.

Henry's experience of abuse was in a totally different context, but its effects have been just as profound:

> I was never raped by either of my abusers. I would describe it as my private parts being interfered with. It immediately felt wrong and made me feel awkward and embarrassed. Looking back now, there were a whole lot of symptoms that came from being abused that I thought were all of my own making. On the one hand I was shocked to discover that my abuser had put all these things on to me. On the other hand I was relieved to think that if these symptoms had been imposed on me, I could also get rid of them through time. There was hope that I could live free of the effects of abuse.

Effects of abuse

In working with abused people I have discovered that sexual abuse can best be understood in terms of its effects upon the person rather than what actually happened, as illustrated by Heather and Henry's accounts. Humans are born with different predispositions in regard to handling trauma. The awfulness of the abuse should not be underestimated of course, but a person's reaction to it has to be the starting place for helping any abused person. As a counsellor, I have known people who have experienced few symptoms after sexual abuse although their story may have sounded horrendous. How anyone reacts to the pain of abuse is to some extent dependent on past influences in life, such as the type of family and upbringing; life experience to date; the degree of maturing as a person that has taken place before and since the abuse; and how well life is coped with in general. For instance, a person brought up in a family where there were few expressions of love would probably react differently to someone brought up in a more loving environment.

In the case of young children, it has to be borne in mind that for a child, whatever happens to them is accepted as 'normal' – they have no wider framework within which to assess the normality of their experience. Flora, a lady who only began to experience difficulties regarding her childhood experience of abuse in her thirties, observes: 'I am constantly being taken by surprise by other people's reactions to my story, and am gradually realising the enormity of what happened to me, partly through their response.' It is this distortion of healthy normality that makes the sexual abuse of young children so particularly abhorrent. It deprives children of the right to a normal childhood and fails to respect their integrity as individuals.

All sexual abuse is wrong because it hurts the person:

- physically;
- psychologically;
- emotionally;
- sexually;
- relationally;
- by causing confusion, fear, anger, shame and self-blame;
- by depriving people of the right to decide what happens to their own body.

Games abusers play

Abusers frequently employ strategies to blackmail the abused person into fearful complicity and silence. Here are some of the tactics I have had related to me over the years by abused people I have counselled:

- This is our little secret. No one else will understand.
- Nobody will believe you.
- Don't tell your mother or it will make her ill/she will go away/she will be angry with you/she will kill you/she will kill me...

- Don't tell or you will be put into care/I will be put in jail...
- If you tell I'll just get another little boy/girl/I won't love you any more/I'll give you a spanking/ thrashing/I'll kill you/I'll kill your dog...
- Everything will be all right if you just don't tell.

Abusers may also use expressions that sound innocent enough, and that anyone might say to a child, but which in the mouth of an abuser become a form of emotional blackmail. Some of the following comments may sound familiar to someone who has been abused:

- This is our little game...
- I'll let you watch TV late if...
- Come and I'll show you the tickling game.
- You're my special girl/boy.
- It's okay, everybody does it.
- This is something special we do because we love each other.
- I'll give you sweets/money if...
- I'll buy you a bike/puppy if...
- What's the matter? Don't you like me?

When a child is involved the abuser is usually clever enough to make sure that no one else is around when such things are said. He or she begins the relationship by relating to the child in seemingly normal ways, such as being friendly and kind, and taking an interest, resulting in the child being confused about the abuser's behaviour once abuse enters the relationship. An example, which is quite common, is when an abuser offers to help the child to learn a sport or play a musical instrument – such activities require spending time alone with the child and the parents' permission is secured.

I have often come across situations where an abused person was taught, for example, that love means hate. So when a non-abusive person says, 'I love you', the child would understand it to mean, 'I hate you'. The child is then constantly on their guard for what horrendous thing is about to happen to them, because the abuser has polluted these normally innocent words for them. Not surprisingly, a child who is sexually abused could well experience confusion and a lack of trust in other relationships; similar comments from a non-abusive person could sound threatening because of how the abuser's words were twisted to accommodate abuse. Words or phrases can become fear-inducing triggers.

Who's to blame?

It is utterly normal for an abused person to want to take the blame, but from the outset, as a counsellor, I must make my position clear – a sexually abused person has been wronged and is not the one who should feel guilty. The responsibility for abusing always lies with the abuser. This is a real sticking point with many abused people, who invariably feel that they are responsible in some way for the abuse happening in the first place, or for the abuse continuing. It is normally the abuser's intention to make the abused person feel responsible for what is wrong, since no abuser wishes to be found out. The abused person will then stay silent out of guilt or fear. An abuser wants to be able to continue abusing and will use any deceit or lies to further that end.

In the eyes of the law, where child abuse is concerned, the adult is always the one with greater power, authority and knowledge; therefore the adult has to take the responsibility and blame for the abuse. Abuse is about power and not just about sex.[11] Children do not expect adults to harm them and have every right to expect that they will be safe in adult

---

11. See more in chapter 7.

company. A former client of mine was made to feel responsible for the abuse of other siblings, because she did not comply with her abuser's wishes. She felt under tremendous pressure to allow herself to be abused so that other family members might be spared such an ordeal. Tragically, as she looked back, she could see that her seeming 'willingness' to respond did not in fact spare anyone else.

It is all too easy for an abuser to persuade a child that there is nothing wrong and that they should not tell. Indeed, children may not always realise at the time that there is anything wrong. By nature, children are trusting, and in a non-abusive situation this trust is normal and well placed. Also, when they are very young, children have not developed sexually and still have a childish innocence about what is or is not appropriate behaviour. The sense of responsibility for what happened, or of having enjoyed it to some extent, can become a terrible burden in later life.

Where does God fit in?

If the fact of being abused is acknowledged, people who have been abused will often question why it happened to them, and speculate on what might have been: 'If only the abuse had never happened ... if only I hadn't been there at the time ... if only I had seen it coming ... if only I had stopped it.' They frequently blame themselves, and are weighed down by thinking they need to take on the responsibility. Also abused people may doubt whether there is a God at all, particularly if they have prayed for the abuse to stop, and nothing seemed to change. They may very well ask, 'Where was God in all of this? Didn't he care?' Flora asked this very question:

I once had a very moving experience when I cried out to God, 'Where were you when this happened to me?' and then had a vision of Jesus hanging on the cross, right beside me in the garage where the assault took place – dying to set me free from the consequences of someone else's sin. However, I have to say that there are times when this does not seem to me like an adequate response.

As a Christian, my response to these questions would be that the God of all the earth loves each and every one of us and that he grieves over the pain that so many people have to suffer. It was never his plan or purpose that sexual abuse should be anybody's experience.[12] Christians believe that the Bible is the authoritative Word of God and is relevant to their lives. God's promise is to never leave us, but to stay with us in and through any and every experience. 'Do not be afraid or terrified because of them, for the LORD your God goes with you; he will never leave you nor forsake you' (Deut. 31:6). That does not always mean deliverance from harm in this life.

Society today regards child sexual abuse as particularly abhorrent, and rightly so, but it is not unique to the present day. Abuse certainly goes back to biblical times.[13] As the Bible says, 'There is nothing new under the sun' (Eccles. 1:9). The good news of the Christian gospel is that there is indeed a God who sees all that happens in this world, and who cares. Whatever a person's perception, there is the certainty that there is a God who cares so much that he got personally involved with all of mankind. The birth, life, death and resurrection of Jesus Christ, God's only Son, has demonstrated once and for all time God's commitment to the world and to individuals. Jesus died and rose again for each one of us over 2,000 years ago. What greater proof could there be of his concern for each and every person in this world?

---

12. See more in chapter 5.
13. Judges 19:22-30. This is a sordid tale involving abuse, rape, kidnap and murder. 2 Samuel 13, especially verses 7-14 records incest.

God does work miracles, and can at times affect immediate healing. More usually, however, healing from sexual abuse is a process, and sometimes a very slow one. Over the years, I have watched God's quiet but significant intervention in the healing of every kind of torn emotion that abused people suffer. In my experience every inch of healing is a miraculous event. God knows how much healing anyone can cope with at any given time, and I am a great believer in allowing God to raise the issues that someone is ready to deal with at the time they can cope with them and not a minute earlier.[14] Of course it is natural to want immediate relief from pain, but that might be more than most people (and perhaps their families) could cope with, given the radical adjustments in attitudes and beliefs about themselves and God that are often required. God usually heals by dealing with difficulties layer by layer, and as the one who created us, knows what is best.

It is understandable that one's image of God becomes tarnished and unhealthy through suffering sexual abuse. An abused person may feel that God is not trustworthy. For instance, a man who has been abused by his father might struggle to see God as a loving Heavenly Father. Because of what was done to him, his perception might be that God is to be feared. He might therefore not know how to receive God's love or how to relate to God in a healthy way.[15] One man I worked with became a Christian long after his abuse came to an end. When he realised God must have been there at the time of his being abused, he became angry that God had not openly intervened. It then occurred to him that the abuse he suffered could have been much worse. He also remembered that God gave each of us freedom of choice and that his abuser had chosen to sexually

14. See more in chapter 4.
15. See more in chapter 5.

abuse him; it was not what God had wanted or chosen for our client. He was also clear that God did not hold him responsible for the abuse. He began to appreciate that he too had made choices in his life that had hurt other people, even though he had never abused anyone and would never want to. Our client asked God to forgive him for all he had done wrong, and he found healing through the process of facing the truth about God's love for him as an individual and about God's grief that he had suffered at the hands of an abuser.

Both Heather and Henry have discovered God's power to help and heal their past hurts. Their stories continue to unfold later in this book, as we explore further the topics touched on in this chapter.

A person's view of God may be affected particularly badly if the abuser was a Christian, and this may also affect how Christianity and the church are perceived. Christian counsellors need to be especially sensitive in dealing with this topic. Sadly it has to be acknowledged that sometimes church can be a place of wounding and hurt instead of healing and peace. Christians too can and do abuse. This in no way suggests that God's help is defective or that he has abandoned them; it reflects the failure of Christians to live in obedience to God's Word and to walk daily in God's will.[16] Unless churches have good vetting procedures in place in conjunction with child protection policies, it can be all too easy for abusers to become trusted people who can easily get close to children. In fact, without adequate safeguards being in place, those who seek an inappropriate relationship with children, which might include sex, often have a good chance of becoming trusted in a church context, and of having close contact with young people. Writing about this particular problem, one Christian commentator,

---

16. The complex reasons why anybody abuses are addressed in chapter 7.

Rebecca Newman, says:

> If I could give one message to the church I am part of in this country, I would ask it to stop being so naïve about abuse... It is time we woke up to the stark reality that in our congregations there are people who are currently being abused. There are men and women worshipping with us who are abusing their own children or others in their care.[17]

It is perfectly possible that the delightful and pleasant person sitting in the pew Sunday by Sunday, could be leading a double life.

Today, in mainstream churches, Child Protection Policies are now in place to enable them to adopt good practice with regard to people working with children. However, since this will only pick up those whose abusive behaviour has been reported, it will be of little use unless churches also take care to avoid situations where workers are alone with children. Hopefully good policies and practices will go a long way to discourage abusers in a church context. Churches need to talk openly about abuse and create a place where abused people feel it is acceptable to talk about inner pain. Increasingly, churches need to know how to help, respond and support those who have been sexually abused, or, indeed, those who have suffered any other form of abuse.

Truth brings freedom

Someone who has been sexually abused often submerges deep feelings of having been injured and wounded beneath some sort of appearance of normality, either consciously or subconsciously. If a time comes when those feelings begin to bubble up to the surface, they should not be feared. They can be faced

---

17. Rebecca Newman, *Releasing the Scream* (Hodder and Stoughton, London, 1994, p. 169).

step by step with loving support, specialist help if required, and a growing trust and belief in God's power to help.

Facing the truth that there has been abuse is the first step (although not necessarily an easy one) towards getting well and in moving towards freedom. Freedom is surely the goal of any abused person – to be free of the damaging effects of abuse. Facing the repercussions of sexual abuse allows an abused person to emerge with greater self-understanding, and the capacity to move forward into the freedom that truth brings. It also leads the abused person to begin to feel normal and to become a well-integrated person.

It is to be hoped that the reader will increase in hope for life beyond sexual abuse through the reading of this book. In the next chapter we look at how the emotions are affected by abuse, and the defences adopted to prevent further hurt. Chapter 3 looks at the catalogue of symptoms that abuse can produce and offers some suggestions as to how to deal with them. Then in chapter 4 we look at ways forward by discussing the topic of trust, the dignity of every human being and the need for a healthy self-image. Relating to God is discussed in chapter 5. Chapter 6 looks at relating to other people, including family, along with the rewards that come from wholesome relating. The final chapter looks at the issue of damaged sexuality and considers what drives people to be abusers. The book concludes with a message of hope.

CHAPTER 2

SURVIVAL TECHNIQUES

An emotional web

No words can adequately describe the implications of abuse and the damage that sexual abuse leaves behind in a person. Sexual abuse causes brokenness at various levels and people react in different ways, but it is clear that the many pressures and issues that come from sexual abuse can affect both the personality and relationships. Sometimes the pain and the feelings are very deep within the person's heart, often coming to the surface through flashbacks or nightmares replicating the abuse. Those feelings often gnaw away inside, and the person increasingly feels the need to scream as a means of release from the very profound pain of these feelings. That scream often has to be inward and silent because of the fear that once such deep pain starts to be expressed, it might become unmanageable, or that if a scream was actually let out, there might be no one there to help. So what actually happens is a build–up of intense inner pain. Without any release for the pressure, together with the fear of what might happen and of losing control, the person may feel ready to explode. The 'silent screams' must be listened to and dealt with, however, or they may, in time, make the person ill. Such illness can make life intolerable.

The brokenness caused by abuse covers a whole range of emotions. The following list of words may begin to describe some of the feelings an abused person might experience: brokenness, disintegration, dysfunction, shame, dirt, blame, self-hate, condemnation, mistrust, hate, bewilderment, frustration, confusion, anger, rage, grief, pain, trauma. In addition there may be a wrong and distorted image of God, self-image problems, a desire to suffer further abuse or violence, sickness or revulsion as a result of what has happened, confusion over sexual identity.

Relating to others can be particularly challenging and confusing for an abused person. These relational difficulties may be characterised by the avoidance of intimacy, fear of abandonment and an inability to trust others, even those trying to help. This may be particularly pronounced when there have been elements of or direct examples of collusion in a relationship. Collusion can be either explicit or implicit. Explicit collusion is when two people agree to keep secrets; implicit collusion occurs when there is an unspoken conspiracy between two parties, as may be the case when someone knows about an abusive situation but fails to address it. For example, I once knew a mother who was aware her husband was abusing their three children but was not emotionally equipped to face it, share this knowledge with anyone or report it to the authorities. Her husband knew that she was aware of the situation, but they never spoke to each other about it. As a result the children were in an abusive home for many years before someone else reported the situation. The father was eventually imprisoned for his behaviour and all three children have ongoing contact with their mother.

My heart goes out to abused people, whether they suffered in the past or the present. From my experience as a counsellor, a large number of commonly experienced difficulties need dealing with in the lives of sexually abused people. These can include: frozen feelings; fear of authority figures; continuing physical and or verbal abuse; an expectation of problems; adopting excessive responsibility, emotional turmoil and constant guilt. Needless to say, even a few of these things can lead to a feeling of being trapped in a tangled web, and there is a tendency for people to feel that they are falling deeper and deeper into despondency and despair. Their emotions may be out of control and defences may be put in place that say loudly, 'I have been hurt enough and have no intention of being hurt any more.' Thinking may be confused, and people frequently have problems in knowing how to make wise decisions, being either overly passive or indecisive, or too determined and impulsive. Attempting to do very ordinary things can take an incredible amount of energy for abused people; in fact, small tasks can seem enormous, because of the damage done to their entire being and the effort required to survive from moment to moment.

There are often layers of symptoms and seemingly over-whelming emotions that need to be disentangled, and even then the person may not fully understand or remember the whole story. It is all too easy either to bury emotions or to focus on them in an unhelpful way. In the case of someone who has suffered sexual abuse, feelings may have been buried or frozen at the time of the abuse, and much sensitivity is needed when trying to draw alongside anyone suffering in this way. Even when a person can identify and acknowledge how they feel, the pain may still be present. Being able to name the pain does not in itself cure the problem. Feelings are a gift from God, indicating that something is going on inside – but they are not always a reliable guide as to how to respond.

Coping Strategies

During the last twenty years I have heard countless tales, each one heartbreaking. I am at a loss to know how to describe the devastation and destruction my clients must feel inside. I am also at a loss to put into words the untold agony, the layers of pain, the sense of self having been shattered into smithereens and the sure conviction abused people have that their lives will never be any better than at present. However, I never cease to be amazed at the capacity for human beings to suffer in the most appalling ways and yet survive.

So how do people survive the emotional turmoil and pain? Many find ways to cope, either consciously or subconsciously. These strategies can be surprisingly effective – at least for a while. As we look at some of these strategies, it is vitally important to realise that they are not unique to people who have suffered sexual abuse; these strategies can as easily be used to cope with the pain of quite different experiences and problems. Just because someone uses a number of these coping strategies, it does not therefore follow that he or she has been sexually abused at some time.

The art of suppression

As has already been mentioned, abused people often learn to cry silently and to scream silently, to push back every emotion for fear of being overwhelmed by the force of the feelings. This can have its dangers, as I have pointed out above, but it does enable people to survive, both during and after abuse. I have had to deal with a lot of anger that has welled up in myself over the years as I have listened to 'children', now grown up, recounting their sufferings at the hands of those who should have loved them. What an outrage that children should have to suffer in this way! These children had to scream silently because there was no one they could turn to, or in some cases, no --one they thought they could turn to. Even worse is the thought that some did try to explain what was happening to them, only to find that they were not listened to, not understood or not believed. It is a terrible indictment of our society that these children were so little respected that there was no one to whom they could turn, and were often failed by those to whom they did turn for help.

Sexual abuse can cause a numbness, an inability to cry, or even an inner vow which goes something like this, 'I will not cry, I will not show them how much it hurts.' It amazes me how often people come for counselling and sit calmly telling me the facts of their abuse as though they were recounting a story that had never touched their emotions. A real detachment can exist; they can appear to have no feelings as they recount horrific abuse, their faces betraying nothing of what has happened to them; they are blank, detached and expressionless. Those who are abused learn through bitter experience that revealing their emotions does not usually stem the flow of abuse, and may actually make it worse, particularly if the abuser is a sadist or driven by a need to exercise his power. Not surprisingly, denying or suppressing the emotions becomes a necessary defence mechanism. Amazingly, it is quite common for people to be completely unaware of the emotions of the heart and to function very well in certain situations. It is perfectly possible for emotions to be frozen due to the effects of abuse. Our minds are 90% subconscious, so we have the capacity to store a huge amount in our minds without having ready access to it.

The art of regression
Many of my clients have tried to cope with the horror of their abuse by not facing up to their own growth as a person and choose to remain a child despite growing in years and stature. Psychologists understand regression to be a returning to a

particular point in a person's development, which is not the person's clear-minded, mature state, but one which is brought about by trauma, and involves a disconnection from the self. To regress creates distance from other people, and in a severe form can lead to mental illness. Being a 'child' or going backwards in time can feel safer and more secure than facing the responsibilities and pressures of adulthood. This regression is probably a heart's cry to go back to a time when life was perceived as being safe and before the abuse occurred. It is an understandable defence or strategy subconsciously designed to take away some of the emotional pain. It may show itself in behaviour which is generally immature, or may become evident only with particular people or in particular circumstances, when it becomes a defensive or evasive protective strategy. An example of this would be a lady I once worked with who, at times when it felt safer, would begin to speak like a small child instead of the adult that she was. Through counselling it became clear that this was a defensive regression, designed to avoid any present–day responsibility. She was not willing to face responsibility and so became the hurting child in order to avoid it. As counselling progressed I heard less and less of the child and more of the adult.

The art of forgetting

Because our minds are so complex, it is perfectly possible for people to 'forget' for many years that they have been abused and to suppress that memory so profoundly that it becomes locked into the subconscious and is not consciously retrievable. It is a recognised reaction to trauma that facts and feelings can be locked into the subconscious for a considerable time. As human beings, we seem to have the capacity to forget pain and trauma. Sometimes, when the memories begin to surface, they can seem more like a dream than reality. These true memories can be triggered at a much later date by a seemingly trivial incident and when least expected.

A lady I worked with many years ago seemed to be getting on well in her life, in all areas, when a memory unexpectedly surfaced. The initial memory was of being made to pose for sexual photographs, and later she remembered that as a youngster she was also forced to witness sexual acts. It troubled her greatly that she had 'forgotten' what had happened to her. There was considerable comfort for her when she discovered during counselling that forgetting the trauma is a very common way for a child to handle the pain. In remembering, she had the opportunity to look at the pain and then go on to deal with it.

Faulty memories

It is quite possible for the mind to play tricks; people can experience false memories. A false memory is when something is 'remembered' that is not accurate or which never happened. This can be the traumatised mind's way of blocking out an actual trauma, which in reality is something worse than the false memory. On the other hand, the false memory may not be right in any way and would be indicative of some other problem, such as, for instance, a need for greater attention or not being listened to. Clearly it would be wonderful if the person discovered that he or she had not been abused after all. However, one needs great discernment and skill to distinguish between false memories and actual abuse.

There are conflicting views about this problem, which has been labelled 'false memory syndrome'. Dr John F. Kihlstrom, professor of psychology at Yale University, has suggested the following definition of what is called False Memory Syndrome:

[A] condition from which a person's identity and interpersonal relationships are centered around a memory of traumatic

41

experience which is objectively false but in which the person strongly believes. Note that the syndrome is not characterized by false memories as such. We all have memories that are inaccurate. Rather the syndrome may be diagnosed when the memory is so deeply ingrained that it orients the individual's entire personality and lifestyle, in turn disrupting all sorts of other adaptive behavior. The analogy to personality disorder is intentional. False Memory Syndrome is especially destructive because the person assiduously avoids confrontation with any evidence that might challenge the memory. Thus it takes on a life of its own, encapsulated and resistant to correction. The person may become so focused on memory that he or she may be effectively distracted from coping with the real problems in his or her life.[1]

It is thought that 'closed questions' can raise up false memories by indicating in the question the answer that is expected. A closed question is one that can be answered by one word, a phrase or a platitude, and often they don't help in understanding the person. Closed questions often begin with words like 'do', 'are', 'is' or 'have': for instance, 'Do you feel dreadful about this?' The only answer to that is either 'yes' or 'no'. It stops the abused person from talking freely. Open questions are the opposite. They cannot be answered by a single word or phrase and encourage the person to go on telling their story: for instance, 'Tell me how that makes you feel?' or 'Describe what you experienced more fully for me?' Emotionally distressed people can be especially susceptible to suggestion, and if the possibility is put to them that past abuse is the cause of their present woes, this can have devastating consequences. If the person begins to find 'memories' to support the view that abuse has occurred, it could have serious repercussions

---

1. From www.stopbadtherapy.com.

for existing relationships with supposed 'abusers', particularly if they are family members, and leave the real causes of the person's difficulties unresolved.

Sometimes someone comes along for counselling who has a group of symptoms or signs which, taken together, has led that person, or someone else, to believe that sexual abuse has occurred. In actual fact, because the symptoms and signs are sometimes misinterpreted, abuse may not have taken place and that means there is another problem altogether, which needs to be looked at.

I will never forget a lady I shall call Elizabeth. Her distress was overwhelming when her daughter accused her of sexually abusing her as a youngster and refused her access to her grandchild. Elizabeth was consistently adamant that she had never harmed her daughter in this way, and was seeking to clear her name. The grief in Elizabeth was severe and she suffered greatly as a result of this false accusation. It took three years for her daughter to break her silence. When she did, Elizabeth was staggered at what she heard. Her daughter wrote to her and explained in a long letter that because of another trauma in her life she had misunderstood some of her early years. Apparently Elizabeth's daughter got very drunk one night and spoke about childhood abuse. Then she went for help, and although she had no conscious memory of having being abused, felt that this must have indeed happened. After three years of no contact with her mother and three years of intensive help and support from professionals, Elizabeth's daughter came to the realisation that abuse had never actually occurred. Her letter was full of apologies and of the expectation that her mother would now not be willing to be in touch with her. In fact, Elizabeth was overjoyed and through a process of planned meetings was able to fully restore relations with her daughter and her granddaughter. It goes without saying that this is not always the outcome when abuse is presumed to have taken place.[2]

Another kind of 'false memory' can occur as a result of an exceptionally vivid dream about an abusive incident. I have known people who have had this experience, and who became convinced that the dream must have actually happened at some previous time in their life. This is not necessarily true, of course, because dreams are primarily of our own creation and offer insight into a person's attitudes and feelings towards his or her own experience of life. For instance, if a person read about a terrible abuse incident and then dreamt it happened to him or her, this could be because they were imagining what it must be like, not because it was something actually experienced. Hence it may not be wise to interpret dreams literally, but probably more helpful to see them as representative of aspects of our past or present experience; in other words they are symbolic not real.

To quote from Russ Parker's book *Healing Dreams*:

> A snake in a dream may mean to one person something evil or demonic, as the story of the garden of Eden in the book of Genesis may imply (Gen. 3:1, 14); to another person it may symbolize healing because it is used as a badge by some branches of the health service, and also may recall the story of the Israelites looking towards the brazen serpent of Moses for a cure for the affliction brought on by disobedience to God (Num. 21:8). It would be all too easy to redirect the dream along the line of our own understanding of symbols, and thus fail to understand the dream at all.[3]

2. For help with false memories contact the British False Memory Society, Bradford-on-Avon, Wiltshire, England, BA15 1NF, Tel. 01225 868682. Web www.bfms.org.uk. For international contact details see appendix.
3. Russ Parker, *Healing Dreams*, Triangle, London, 2000.

Since accurate interpretation of dreams is not always possible, great caution is needed.

Living in unreality

Emotional pain can often be covered up rather than dealt with. For instance, for a child in an incestuous relationship, unreality can be an escape route, because for them there is no place to run, no one to speak to, no way out. What is real can be altogether too painful to consider or bear. Fear, coupled with an intense false loyalty to an abuser, can lead to a denial of facts, an ignoring of reality and a belief in unreality, no matter how incredible that may be. To complicate matters, there can be an elaborate web or matrix of half truths that allow groups of people to ignore what is blatantly true and real, for instance, family members, churches and colleagues.

A reaction to the fearful situation she found herself in caused one client, when she was a wee girl who had severe ongoing abuse to contend with, to truly believe she was a fairy rather than the girl who was being abused. This 'splitting' of identity helped the child to feel she could cope, and she could then believe the abuse wasn't happening to her. This was a coping strategy where the child was adopting a way of thinking to make her feel safer.

Splitting of the personality can lead an abused person to ignore his or her own breaking heart, and even to regard the one who has broken it as a saint who couldn't possibly do harm. Believing the fantasy becomes a way of life and can feel more comfortable than the truth. In fact, the abused person can become so familiar with the fantasy story–line, that it can become more real than the reality. This unreal world becomes a 'safe place'. The fantasy can take on a life of its own, and be carefully nurtured. When splitting of a person is adopted in a major way, that person can develop a multiple personality disorder, sometimes known as disassociative disorder. This is where two or more distinct personalities apparently exist in one individual. It has to be acknowledged that this is a disorder that can trouble those who have been severely abused. Specialist help is needed and can be provided by doctors, psychiatrists and experienced counsellors.

I once counselled someone I shall call Pat, who lived in fear of her life because of the abuse she had suffered at the hands of an organised paedophile ring. By the time Pat came for counselling she had at least four recognisable personalities, or characters. They all spoke differently, had different names and related in a variety of ways. One character was a child, and she seemed to be the age the girl was when the sexual abuse began; another was a teenager and reacted in adolescent ways. The goal of counselling was to help Pat live with her characters integrated and at one with each other. Pat never chose to be anybody other than herself and yet found that a thousand different things could trigger one of her other characters to come to the fore. Each time we met, I took her as she was that day. If she was adolescent, then I would deal with the teenage issues that were troubling her. When Pat was adult and more like 'herself', we would talk about the other 'characters'. She would often laugh at what they had been saying. Pat was keen to see all the fragmentations of her personality merge as one and this happened as she dealt with the abuse issues. As peace grew within, she integrated in small but significant ways. There was no long–term need to have the 'child' or 'adolescent' playing tantrums because they were fully heard and understood in the emotionally safe place of counselling. The 'child' would be helped in one counselling session and that eased the burden on the adolescent and the adult. Pat is still aware of time that she can't account for, when other fragments of her personality dominated and Pat herself, as the adult, did not have such a clear memory of what they said or did. These times are getting less. It seemed to help that I was unperturbed by which one of Pat's characters turned up for counselling on any given day.

The art of denial

People need strategies to deal with the pain of abuse, and one of them is to deny that it ever happened in the first place, or that it is untrue. Denial goes one stage deeper than unreality. The abused person has been hurt and damaged enough and wants to be surrounded by defences in order to avoid further internal suffering. Denial is a preferred route for many whose pain is so deep that it feels incurable, and is often successful over many years. It can be, and indeed often acts as, a survival mechanism. As a counsellor, I can quite understand that denial has its uses. For someone who has been sexually abused, there can be tremendous pain in being honest about what really happened. Denial is neither deliberate deception nor a particular weakness. Rather it is a way of coping and becomes a way of life, engrained in the personality.

Secrecy and denial can become a way of life for some people who have been abused. Shame silences the person, as does the abuser, who has probably demanded that nothing be said about the abuse because he or she has no desire to be found out or to lose the opportunity to abuse in the future. To add further complications, denial can be part of an unhealthy pattern existing within a family. An example of what I mean would be a family where the real issues are never spoken about and the truth is never faced. This can, of course, be true of abusive and non-abusive families! Many topics of conversation become no-go areas, placing a restriction on what is regarded as safe to talk about. Surface conversations are therefore the norm. This is like an unwritten rulebook, whereby family members know intuitively what they can and cannot speak about. Denial therefore is heaped upon denial.

The possibility of denying the truth to one's self is also fuelled by some popular myths:

- abuse only happens in some sectors of society;
- it's only people who are raped who have really been sexually abused;
- my symptoms are mild in comparison to others, so I'll ignore them just now;
- if I bury how I feel I won't ever need to deal with this
- abuse doesn't happen amongst Christians.

After a while, maybe years later, denial may have served its purpose. It may become too difficult to keep pushing down the pain, to ignore what is staring the abused person in the face and to believe everything is going well, when something is obviously very wrong.

Patterns of unhelpful behaviour involving denial have to be broken or they will continue repeating themselves, possibly through generations to come. That is not to say that those who have been abused will necessarily go on to abuse others, but reactions to abuse can sometimes affect the next generation, causing a predisposition to similar behaviour. In other words, unresolved pain can affect other people.

However, it must be emphasised that usually denial and re-pression do not work in the long term when it comes to emo-tions. People need to find strategies that allow them to face and acknowledge their emotions, whilst at the same time dealing with them. A way needs to be found that allows someone who has been damaged emotionally to experience and face their emotions without sinking beneath the weight of them.

Time for reality

By the time people come for counselling, they have usually gone beyond the point where these coping strategies are helping them. Most will realise that they need to face up to reality.

Heather's experience may help to describe what it can involve to get to that point of wanting reality. She explains the denial and unreality that were around in her life for a long time:

Denial was my bread and butter, all part of living a lie, pretending to myself for the most part that this thing couldn't have happened to me. Bad things only happen to bad people therefore I must be bad. I couldn't believe that my abuser would do anything bad to me. He loves me, he surely must. He is my daddy after all. He's meant to love me. No, it must have been something I did. I was only young at the time. I wonder what I could have done?

Looking back at the family scene, I had absolutely no conscious notion that I was in denial; that went on for years. I could watch an abuse documentary on television and it didn't touch me because it didn't apply to me, or so I thought. Denial was part of my daily routine. My family all pretended they were happy, and it was easy to pretend because we all played the same game. I didn't know it was a game. I thought it was reality.

Only gradually, over many years, did the truth dawn on me and the pain of it creep into the deepest recesses of my heart. And I began the long, hard road of facing the truth. Could I cope with what was gradually becoming reality – did I have the strength? Would I survive if I consciously believed something which no one else was saying? I was hoping somebody might ask me if I had ever been abused, but no one ever did. It came to me slowly. I began by picking up the pieces, and when I had put them all together, I didn't like what I saw. I resisted and said to myself, 'Why should I believe this? It will turn my entire world upside down.' The big trouble for me was that I couldn't let anyone know what I was thinking. Such exposure would have been too much for me at this stage. Maybe I wouldn't survive if I believed what I was wondering. What effort and time I have put into wondering – just wondering, 'Is it possibly true?' The relief and inner torment, such a mixture of emotions, was considerable once I decided that, yes, it is true that I have been abused. The daddy who was meant to love me, abused me. Maybe I wasn't lovable? Well, I could console myself with the fact that he didn't rape me. It could have been much worse. Relief came ... but at the same time a dark cloud descended upon me with such clarity that I became a bit frightened. Maybe if I let it all sink down inside it will never re-emerge.

Heather's internal debate with herself about who was responsible, who was to blame, and about whether or not her abuser loved her, may be familiar to anyone who has been abused. Heather swings in and out of reality and minimises the facts in order to make herself feel better. She is plagued by self-doubt and shame.

Heather reached a point in her life when she had to face up to the truth and reality, painful though that was. The failure to recognise what had happened in the past led to a variety of difficulties in her life, which she could not understand and deal with until she had acknowledged the nature of the abuse she had suffered. As Heather's story illustrates, the experience of remembering long–suppressed memories can be traumatic, and such flashbacks of the abuse can come a long time after the event.

CHAPTER 3

A CATALOGUE OF PAIN

The experience of sexual abuse can affect the way people feel and behave in a variety of ways. Abuse – any abuse – can have devastating consequences, and the effects of abuse in a person's life cannot be quantified solely by what took place. I believe someone can be seriously harmed by what might be regarded as a minor abusive incident. In my experience, it is not so much what actually happens to a person that matters, but rather the impact and consequences on feelings and behaviour. As we have seen, people who have been abused may deny or suppress the reality of their experience. Yet whether this is done consciously or subconsciously, people's behaviour and attitudes may betray that they have been hurt. People may unconsciously rely on behaviour and thinking that dulls the pain, enabling them to cope, or so they think. Such 'defences' can include denial: pretending the situation doesn't exist; shifting the blame to someone else; rationalising it away; 'logically' explaining away the symptoms and their root cause; regressing into childhood patterns; or turning to smoke screens like alcohol, drugs or food. Maintaining a position of denial or suppression can absorb a tremendous amount of emotional energy and be immensely draining.

Reactions to sexual abuse are so complex that any one or more of a wide range of symptoms may need to be addressed. The symptoms described below are those I have encountered most frequently in the course of counselling sexually abused clients. I quote the experience of some of these clients, with permission, to convey the impact of these symptoms in their experience more effectively. Given the very diverse reactions that people experience to sexual abuse, an abused person might not recognise some, or indeed any, of these symptoms as being part of his or her experience. That would be a cause for rejoicing! Equally, anyone reading this chapter might be aware of experiencing one or more of the symptoms. However, it is important to realise that all or any of the symptoms mentioned in this chapter can just as easily be part and parcel of life for people who have never been sexually abused; they may be the result of other life experiences.

For someone who has been sexually abused, the number and intensity of symptoms experienced can seem overwhelming, but there really is hope for healing – I have seen it happen in people's lives so often. Each symptom can be faced and dealt with and the person can move on to a better life beyond abuse. Freedom from symptoms is the ultimate goal in counselling, although there may be layers of symptoms that only become apparent after the most immediately obvious ones have been dealt with. For that reason healing can be a long process. Nevertheless, from experience I know that healing can be a real possibility over time, and that is why I give suggestions for dealing with each symptom in the list below, in the hope that readers will find these helpful.

Abandonment

'My mother, father, grandparents, abandoned me to my abuser – they were paid to do so. This has left me feeling betrayed, destroyed, shattered and deserted.'

'I was left entirely on my own in the world to raise the child I had as a result of rape.' This girl was only sixteen when she was thrust into motherhood. The feeling of abandonment was very real in her experience, through being left to care for the baby with no support whatsoever.

'I was abandoned when my parents did not believe the youth leader at church had abused me. I was taken into care and a foster family helped me to live again. My parents still relate to my abuser but will have nothing to do with me.' This young man experienced love and care in his foster family and began to relax and feel as though he could live again because he recognised he was in a safe place.

- An abandoned person can be greatly helped by knowing that God is with them and that he never goes away.
- There will be a need for relating to people in a healthy way, even in casual and superficial ways to begin with. Little steps lead to great progress over time. It is a bit like dipping one's toe in the water, taking small steps in relating and trusting another and continuing to do so when this trust is found to be well placed.

Addiction

'It crept up on me unawares. I was a drug addict in a matter of weeks, but it had the distinct advantage of obliterating how I felt about the abuse. One day I may give up, but for now I am content – after a fashion.'

'I discovered that life was far more fulfilling when I gave up alcohol altogether. Admitting I had a problem was the first step. Then I had to learn to walk past pubs and not buy alcohol from shops. Previously alcohol controlled me and had power over me. When I decided to become a Christian I learned that God's power in my life could really help me to resist temptation. My new lifestyle allows me to have real friendships and I am hopeful that I will be able to learn how to relate in more meaningful ways. I'd like a wife, but want to be in full–time employment for another year – just to prove to myself that I am on a new path! I do have struggles, but nothing like before. I have far more good days than bad days.'

- An addict is someone who habitually or compulsively uses anything or anyone to the extent that he or she cannot cope without it.

- Addiction may be evident if there is excessive involvement with a substance, person or relationship and if it involves social or physical harm.

- Breaking the cycle of addiction, especially where it relates to substance abuse, can be very difficult. In this situation specialist help may be needed. Addressing addiction involves overcoming one's powerlessness by accessing a source of power greater than one's own will. Willpower alone is rarely sufficient to break addictive behaviour.

- Details for contacting Alcoholics Anonymous are in the local telephone directory. For Christian help with alcohol issues contact Stauros Foundation, Ballyards Castle, 123 Keady Road Armagh, Northern Ireland, BT60 3AD, Tel. 028 3752 7124. For help with drugs there is the Scottish Drugs Forum in Glasgow on 0141 221 1175 and Know the Score (National Helpline) on 0800 587 5879. National Drugs Helpline is available twenty–four hours a day and can be reached on 0800 77 66 00. Gamblers Anonymous National Helpline is 08700 508880 and the Glasgow office is 0141 630 1033, where there is a twenty–four hour answering service. They will send information packs on kicking the habit if someone phones 07626 947 800. Turning Point offers one–to–one advice, information and counselling for people experiencing substance abuse, either alcohol or drugs. They are available Monday to Friday from 9 am – 5 pm on 0141 427 8200. If someone needs help with glue–sniffing or volatile substances help is available at Re-Solve, 135b Main Street, East Calder, Livingston, Scotland, EH53 0EP, Tel. 01506 881 498. Re-Solve also has a base in England at 30A High Street, Stone, ST15 8AW, Tel. 01785 817885.[1]

Aimlessness

'I had a character change that came about the day I was raped. Before I was purposeful and determined. I knew what my life was about. I had to be hospitalised after the rape and when I came home I did not recognise myself at all. I felt undirected and rootless with no clear way forward in anything.'

- Aimlessness is caused by too much energy being used on painful emotions, leading to no clear view of the future, lack of direction, a shortage of personal goals and ambitions, and of motivation in general.
- Inaccurate beliefs can include, 'I'm not entitled to be happy', 'It is not possible for me to aim for anything', 'My life will not accomplish anything', 'Nothing I do will ever be any good', and 'Anyone I love will always betray me'. Each such belief has to be challenged and countered with an accurate statement once the person realises that his (or her) quality of life is undermined by such attitudes, and that they are completely unjustified. The essential difficulty is that the unhelpful belief has become part of the root problem and seems to keep coming true in the person's life.

---

1. For international contact details see the appendix.

- Healing from aimlessness begins as someone starts to grasp that there is a future and that it can start today. Hope has to be communicated, usually by a person outside of himself or herself.
- Changes in routine and even establishing new interests focuses the mind away from the internal dilemmas and is frequently very beneficial, although it should be recognised that there may be many ups and downs.

Anger

'I was always quietly angry and I covered it with a smile. The anger I had was deep and not accessible. The rage grew and ate away inside of me until I was worried that I would seriously damage someone, because my abuser was no longer alive and I couldn't reach him. My anger then moved on to a new stage, revealing itself in angry episodes, alternating with calm.'

- It is perfectly normal to experience anger after any kind of abuse. Anger can often reveal itself gradually over a long period of time. It may show in a number of ways, ranging from relatively mild emotions, such as displeasure, frustration and disappointment, through rage and anger to increasingly destructive and potentially dangerous ones, such as hatred and uncontrollable fury, which can lead on to revenge.
- Anger can be suppressed and suppressed until it becomes depression associated with denial.
- Anger can be communicated both verbally and non-verbally, by silence, by irritation, by feelings of resentment and bitterness, possibly culminating in hatred of both self and others. It can ultimately lead to violence.
- Unhelpful misconceptions can include – 'I won't be loveable if I am angry'; 'I shouldn't be this angry'; 'If I face this anger, I won't survive.'

- It is important to realise that whilst it is understandable, and even acceptable, to be angry, it is unhealthy to stay angry. Anger has to be dealt with at its roots, by looking into why it has become a major issue. Of course, being abused causes a great deal of internal and external anger. Deciding to deal with the anger, even when it is still felt, is the first step. The next step is to learn to manage anger in legitimate and positive ways rather than being destructive to self or others in actions or words. It helps to be accountable for anger to a person, such as a counsellor or friend; because it will have to be dealt with layer by layer as it comes to the surface.

Anxiety

'I have no fingernails left and my nerves are shot to bits. What if she comes back in the dark when I least expect her? What if it happens again? I can't get on with my life for sheer apprehension and terror at times. I wake up in a sweat and wonder if today will be as bad as yesterday.'

- Anxiety is living in a state of constantly feeling great concern and worry, and an absence of peace.
- This condition can be hard to pin down and recognise in one's self. Other people can usually see it first. Being constantly anxious can lead to depression.
- Anxiety is especially helped by learning to trust, letting go of negative thoughts, and deliberately substituting positive thoughts and pursuing peace in the heart. A question needs to be asked: 'What is hindering ongoing peace in my heart?' Connecting with people in non-threatening arenas, where new friendships and interests can be pursued, can help to shift the focus from self to others, which may ease intense anxiety.

- Developing healthy and supportive relationships will also help the anxious person to productively face his or her anxiety in dialogue with others.

Apathy

'I never seem to get anywhere. The root problem is that an older man in a position of trust abused me. It was like a bomb going off in my head, because since then I can never seem to follow through on anything. I expect life will just go on as before. I would rather other people took the initiative, so I will just do nothing and hope this mess I am in will get sorted.'

- Apathy is a disinclination to engage with life, coupled with a lack of interest or a feeling that it is too risky to engage in meaningful relationships.
- There is no cutting edge in decision making because motivation is at an all time low. This is often the reason why someone allows abuse to continue, or stays in a situation that is causing pain.
- There can be a tendency to withdraw due to lack of energy: 'I need to earn money, but beyond going to work I want to disappear into the wall. I don't have the energy to see people and to have them ask questions.'
- It can be helpful to 'practise' making small decisions and then carry them through. It is vital initially that the decisions arrived at be ones that are possible to achieve, and it may be that someone else will have to suggest attainable goals at first. Building on success helps the person to believe that greater things are possible with time.

Bitterness

'I will never forgive or forget – what they did to me is horrendous and all they deserve is the very worst.'

'It is my belief that I will not be free until my abuser goes to jail. I am very bitter that he has not yet been brought to justice.'

'The world owes me a living because of what happened to me. I will do all I can to extract compensation from the authorities. Then I will feel better.' Sadly money will not release this person from the pain of having been abused.

- Bitterness is akin to anger and is an expression of the intensity of the pain inside. It can cause physical illness as well as strained relationships.
- To be bitter and to remain bitter only causes harm, and will rob the person of health and well-being in the long run.
- Like anger, bitterness is best to be temporary, or it will damage the bitter person.
- Sharing bitterness with a stronger person, perhaps a counsellor, pastor or trusted friend, helps to defuse it, and the other person may offer ideas as to how to resolve the roots of bitterness.

Blame

'I used to sincerely believe the sexual abuse was my fault. I know I was only three at the time, but I thought if I took the blame it could all be sorted. I used to believe that if I just said "sorry" then maybe the pain would go away, but I learned much later on that I wasn't to blame. I then had to face the horror that my daddy was not the perfect man I thought he was.'

'With a lot of pain I faced the truth of who was responsible. It was the little things that seemed to matter most to me – like what he did to my pet. My pet was the only thing I could call my own and he took that away as well. Once I blamed him I was able to see that it wasn't my fault after all

– then I had the genuine option to forgive him. I couldn't have done that if I hadn't blamed him in the first place.' As this lady points out, to forgive is not possible unless the abuser (the person responsible) is blamed for the abuse.

- Blame has to be rightly apportioned. Abused people almost always believe that what happened to them was their own fault. Is the abused person ever to blame for sexual abuse? Never, although they very often feel they are. Children, for example, are never prepared for the event of abuse, so when it happens they often conclude that they have done something bad, or that they are bad. Many abusers say to the child that it is their fault, so they take the blame. Just by virtue of being there, an abuser may claim, the child either made abuse inevitable or precipitated it, yet this is clearly an irrational position, since in the majority of cases involving children, abuse happens with a trusted adult or older person, who has to accept responsibility for the way he or she dealt with temptation. As human beings, we are all liable to be tempted to do what we know to be wrong, but it is only when we give way to temptation that we become culpable.

- Dealing with blame does not involve or justify taking the law into your own hands or taking revenge against the abuser. The abuser needs to take responsibility for his or her wrongdoing by taking the blame, although in reality this may never happen, or the abuser may subsequently deny accepting responsibility. Whatever happens, the abused person needs to be released from falsely taking the blame by working through that false blame and dealing with his or her own issues.

- Much can be gained from concentrating on being re-leased from the implications and symptoms caused by the abuse, rather than remaining burdened with false blame. Great benefits come from forgiving the abuser, because there can then be a moving on from blame to a sense of release through forgiving, whether or not the guilty party takes responsibility. It is not necessary to wait for the abuser to repent of wrongdoing in order to forgive. See *Unforgiveness* and *Forgiveness* in chapter 6.

Confusion

'How did it ever happen? She abused me. Women don't abuse little girls, do they? The more I try and make sense of it, the more confused I get. There's what actually happened, what I think happened and what I want to believe. None of them tie up. I think it all through, don't make sense of it and then go through it all again. It wears me out.'

- Confusion influences how someone feels, how he or she thinks about himself and how he behaves. Often unhelpful decisions can be made while someone is confused, which in turn can create more problems or regrets.
- Confusion drains physical energy levels and burns up an incredible amount of emotional energy. This is how one client described confusion: 'I was lost, disorientated, paralysed and empty.'
- Confusion can be created when sexual feelings, arousal or even orgasm are experienced whilst being abused. Consequently the abused person may feel that they condoned the act or even enjoyed it. This can create great confusion as the person tries to reconcile that with their sense of horror and violation. However, it is important to realise that fear can be a cause of sexual arousal. Equally, the body is designed to be aroused and excited by genital stimulation, so having positive

61

feelings towards the abuser, or being aroused during an abusive situation, does not mean that the person wanted or liked the abuse.

- A useful tool to address confusion is to list one's confused thoughts. Make a list of such thoughts on the left–hand side of a sheet of paper, and in the right–hand column record a clear thought, or a proposed action, designed to sort out the confusion. For example, writing in the left column: 'I don't know and am confused about which job to go for', could be countered with: 'I will seek advice about this confusion from the job centre as soon as I can'. It helps to take small steps, one at a time. Once the right–hand side of such a list is full and has been acted on, no matter how long it takes, there will be a great sense of achievement. Creative writing about any aspect of the turmoil helps to clear the mind. Poetry has the effect of helping to get in touch with emotions. Flora comments, 'In my experience, any creative act brings healing – cross-stitch, bread-making, whatever, as creativity comes from God.'

Contamination

'It was not uncommon for me to have eight baths every day in an attempt to cleanse myself from what was done to me. I went through the same procedure the next day, but it didn't work because I did this every day. The main feeling was that I was spoilt and tarnished or stained, and that it was for life. After counselling and being challenged to face up to who was to blame and whose dirt it was that I was trying to scrub off, I was able to change my behaviour and my thinking. I understood that water wouldn't cleanse me. Moving on with all my issues removed the need for all these baths, and I buy far less soap!'

- Feelings of being dirty, polluted or contaminated as a result of being abused are extremely common. Just knowing this is a common reaction can be helpful in dealing with the overwhelming feelings.
- There is often an inaccurate belief that 'purity is not an option after this abuse'.
- The sense of pollution can make someone feel that no one will ever want to be close to him or her. I have known of people who thought they could never marry because of their overwhelming feelings of contamination.
- The solution is to have a clearer understanding of how to be freed from these feelings by challenging their source. The abused person needs to recognise that the pollution and contamination comes from the abuser, it is not inherent in him or her. Coming into a full realisation and acceptance of the truth about what happened and who is responsible can be releasing in itself. See also *Blame* above.

Denial. see chapter 2.

Depression

'I would never have regarded myself as depressed, but looking back I was. I was single, employed and living independently. Inside my heart was another story. I was broken through sexual abuse and I coped with it by being perfect on the outside. No one would have known. My doctor and counsellor both had a role in helping me find myself again and find health.'

- Depression is a state of dejection or melancholy characterised by feelings of hopelessness and inadequacy. Being depressed can involve loss of perspective, negative thinking, changes in sleeping patterns, either early waking or sleeping all the time, changes in eating habits, loss of the ability to care for oneself (for example, to wash or exercise), feelings of sadness, withdrawal from others yet dissatisfaction with being alone, despair, and loss of hope.

- Depression can affect anyone, at any stage in life, whatever his or her sex or status, whether rich or poor. Many do not recognise their symptoms as depression, but will talk about a 'dark cloud' or a 'shadow' that just won't go away.

- There are several widely recognised types of depression:
    1. Manic depression, or bipolar disorder, which involves alternating periods of elation and depression.
    2. Reactive depression is always in response to an event or series of events.
    3. Endogenous depression grows from within the person and may appear unexpectedly when no known reason for it can be identified. There can sometimes be a physiological reason behind depression, such as thyroid trouble, hormonal issues or a chemical imbalance.

- Sexual abuse almost always affects emotions and can depress the abused person's feelings almost immediately. It can feel like going into automatic pilot. This is a defensive reaction to shock, emotional pain and trauma.

- Depression can be a signal of inner turmoil and as such can be an opportunity to get help. It can be a constructive way to deal with accumulated and unresolved emotions. Depression may require professional help. Even a one–off visit to a doctor can help enormously with diagnosis and possible treatments. Once the root of the depression is identified, a plan can be put together to help the depressed person to get well. Every person has a different route to healing; for instance, one lady I know had to learn to take care of herself physically after feeling depressed for a long time. Medication from her doctor and dealing with her depression with the help of a counsellor enabled her to view her life more positively.

Despair see *Hopelessness.*

Doubts about God
- Doubting God is particularly rife amongst those who have been abused by Christians or people who claim to be religious. See chapter 5 of this book and look into www.runningempty.org for some excellent material on doubting, lack of belief and many other spiritual issues, if you feel like exploring this topic.

Eating disorders
'Five stones in weight and five feet three inches tall. If I lose any more weight I will have to be taken to hospital, they say. Somehow, this doesn't seem to help me to eat. My case appears to be complicated by eating sometimes and not others. The abuse that happened to me involved my mouth and as a result my emotions can be all over the place. If I feel better I can eat, but I just need to remember some of the past and I won't eat for many days.'

- There are a variety of eating disorders that can be triggered off by sexual abuse. It has to be said that other traumatic events can produce the same results, such as family bereavement or break-up, serious illness in the family, leaving home, exams, loss of a close relationship, or bullying. Anorexia, bulimia, binge eating and compulsive overeating are some of the main disorders. These are conditions, which really ought to be addressed, otherwise they may persist, causing permanent damage to health or even becoming life–threatening.

- Eating issues can be rooted in anger, a sense of helplessness or other emotions. Refusing to eat, refusing to stop eating, refusing to keep down food, are all ways of trying to keep control of body shape and life. Refusing to eat can become a habit that masks an unmet need. It is sometimes easier to continue with the habit than to look at the need for change, so the person continues with the familiar and potentially destructive pattern of eating.

- It seems that weight, size, diet, food, anxiety and feelings are all linked in the human psyche in a very complex way. Both comfort eating and refusing to eat can be ways of blocking out painful feelings. There is often a feeling that 'at least I can control this aspect of my life'. One client told me: 'I regard my unwillingness to eat as a form of slow suicide which I have wilfully chosen as a way out of pain.' This girl was not keen to see her past sexual abuse as something that could be addressed and resolved through time because of her general lack of hope.

- Eating disorders can evolve out of years of unhealthy relating and emotional turmoil, so that the emotional pain behind the eating problem needs to be addressed.

- Good nutrition, getting medical and counselling help, quality rest, and gentle exercise are all ways forward. However, obsessive and excessive exercise can be another way of controlling weight, so care needs to be taken in this area.

- Professional help will usually be needed. In the United Kingdom there is the Eating Disorders Association, First Floor, Wensum House, 103 Prince of Wales Road, Norwich, NR1 1DW, www.edauk.com There are also telephone helplines. Adults should phone 0845 6341414; for young people there is Youthline: 0845 6347650. The Eating Disorders Association has an excellent book list.[2]

Fear

'I'm fearful of going out and fearful of staying in. Basically I can't win and fear has got a grip of me.'

'My initial thought was that I could never consider marriage because I would be too fearful of my past coming into the present. I was wrong, because my wife knows all that happened to me and there are no skeletons in the cupboard. We have an honest and loving relationship, so I have nothing to fear. I was honest about my past and every time I remembered something else I spoke openly to my wife.' Fear no longer has such a crippling effect when it is brought into the light.

- Fear can be rational or irrational, helpful or harmful, manageable or unmanageable. It can be attached to any subject matter, but certainly includes the fear of facing the effects of sexual abuse. There can be physical reactions to fearful situations, exhibited in a variety of ways such as skin rashes, headaches, nausea, backache, ulcers, shortness of breath, sleep changes, increased tiredness and loss of appetite. Other physical reactions can be going on which are less easily identified, such as blood pressure fluctuations.

---

2. For international contact details see the appendix.

- At its worst, fear can physically and emotionally paralyse, and any long-term experience of fear can have an adverse effect on someone's quality of life. I will never forget a client who could not forgive herself for not screaming whilst she was being raped. She was convinced that the whole situation was her fault because if she had screamed someone would have come and stopped the rape. In fact she was in no way to blame because fear had completely paralysed her. The simple task of opening her mouth was physically impossible because of the effect of fear, shock and trauma.

- Questions to ask about fear include: what have you feared in the past; what are you fearful of now; what is your greatest fear; what can you or others do to reduce the fear?

- Fear is surmountable, stage by stage. Help from others may be needed to identify what kind of fear it is. The source of fear needs to be broken down into a series of small challenges that can be faced gradually, stage by stage, or it may be that someone else needs to help the person put a sense of perspective on the fear, so that it assumes manageable proportions in the mind.

Grief and Loss

'My childhood innocence was taken from me by my abuser. He robbed me of a great deal. I got well when I learned that it was okay to cry about all I had lost. My grief surfaced at least ten years after the abuse, so it took me by surprise.'

'Grief shocked me by appearing when least expected. It crept up on me by making me feel physically sick. A small issue at work set my emotions off and I became unexpectedly weepy. When I stopped crying the physical ailment had cleared up completely and has never returned. Only later did I realise that grief was working its way through my system, the grief of having been abused as a teenager.'

- Most people expect to experience grief and a sense of loss after the death of someone close to them. They are often unprepared for the various ways in which they may be affected, and for the stages through which a normal experience of grieving may go. Denial, anger, depression and acceptance are all recognised as stages that may be experienced during the grieving process. Bargaining or negotiation can also be part of grief. This is where the abused person enters into some form of negotiation with God or himself or herself. Denial and bargaining often overlap. Denial says the abuse did not happen. Bargaining says the abuse happened but the abused person tries to negotiate that there was no trauma involved. Someone who is bargaining often insists that there should be outside evidence that abuse occurred.

- Grief is deep or intense sorrow, sadness or mourning. All kinds of loss may be experienced through the trauma of sexual abuse: loss of privacy, trust, relationships, childhood, self-acceptance, career, peace, security, freedom, joy, carefreeness, career and perspective. Such losses go deeply into a person's heart, and if left unattended, will not just go away by themselves.

- Choosing to suppress grief is not helpful, so there is a need to grieve the sorrows and losses of the past, to feel them and then let them go. It takes a quantum leap to learn to live without this level of grief in the heart, particularly when it has been a significant part of someone's life for some time.

- It is important to be allowed to grieve, whatever that involves for the individual. Usually this will include facing emotions that may come up in layers, and talking through the different layers of feelings can help. This can only happen at the right time, as feelings can lie dormant for considerable periods of time. Once feelings associated with grief have been worked through, freedom and security will take their place.

Guilt

'I am obsessed with the idea of having been the one to have caused the abuse. It does not help me to know I was only three years of age and my grandfather was in his sixties when he repeatedly visited my bedroom at night. No amount of trying to talk this through has brought me any relief. My counsellor is emphatic that I am not to blame. Although I hear the words, I am still feeling that I must somehow be responsible.'

- Many people I have counselled over the years have felt guilty because they believed it was 'something about me that invited the abuse.' I have frequently heard statements like these: 'I was the kind of child who deserved it', 'I enjoyed the special attention involved, or the rewards, or the money', 'I used the "secret" to get some kind of advantage over the abuser', 'I experienced pleasurable feelings', 'I didn't tell', 'I didn't do enough to stop the abuse', 'I didn't stop my brothers/sisters from being abused', 'by telling I have upset the family/ the neighbourhood/ the church', 'I am responsible for breaking up the family', 'I have brought punishment on the abuser', 'I have had anger towards those who didn't help me', 'I have behaved in destructive or self-destructive ways', and lastly, 'My mum and dad liked him well enough and accepted him.'

- Guilt can be real or imagined, imposed or genuine. Guilt has the potential to distort an abused person's perspective. It is possible to become mentally ill through having never found a solution to guilt. In counselling, guilt and fear are the two symptoms that are most frequently mentioned.

- Identifying guilt is the first step to healing, along with deciding who is actually guilty in the situation. Getting rid of guilt is central to recovery from abuse; however, we need to be sure about whether or not it is true or false guilt we are dealing with.

- False guilt is dealt with by blaming the other person as appropriate. It can be difficult to let go of false guilt because it involves the abused person admitting that he or she was absolutely powerless in the situation. Moving on from realising exactly who was guilty to forgiving the guilty person is tremendously challenging, but can lead to a very deep level of healing for the wronged party.

- Being sorry and seeking forgiveness rectifies real guilt. The Christian believes that guilt and the resulting regret is dealt with at the cross of Jesus, and that forgiveness from God is possible because Jesus took the punishment for our guilt on himself when he died. See *Forgiveness* in chapter 6.

Hatred of self

'I concluded the worst, that I was unlovable and that I was far safer behind my defensive walls. If the definition of "love" is what my abuser kindly did to me when I was only nine, I don't want to know. The term love has lost all meaning for me. As a result I am highly critical about myself.'

- Inaccurate beliefs include – 'I am unlovable, my hatred for myself is justified'; 'No one will ever love me because I am loveless.'

- There is a continuum, beginning with low self-esteem and leading to a lack of self-acceptance that can develop into self-hatred. It is not necessarily connected to harming one's self but may lead the abused person to despise many if not all aspects of his (or her) self: from what they look like to how they deal with challenges, from how they relate to others to how they perform at work, to name but a few examples. This perception of self is provoked by the abuse because the subliminal message is, 'what happened is hateful, therefore I must be despicable and disgusting.'

- Self-hatred is very uncomfortable to live with on an emotional level, but it can also show itself in feelings to do with self-image. Through peer pressure and the media, image has become more and more significant these days, particularly for younger people, for whom the designer label on a garment is all-important. Once a client spoke to me of going to a party feeling she had chosen 'the wrong dress to wear'. Self-image should not be monitored by what the abused person perceives about other people's opinions.

- The way to deal with this problem involves laying aside inaccurate beliefs about one's self, moving towards self-acceptance, being real about personal strengths and weaknesses, learning to cope with one's own company, being honest with one's self and others, and operating within healthy boundaries. See chapter 4 for self-acceptance and chapter 5 for more on boundaries.

Hopelessness and Despair

'At the height of an emotional upset, sadness and despair engulfed me. I could see no way forward. It felt like everything was utterly ruined. This mirrors my general despair. I feel like giving up and see no point in going on.'

'I only went for counselling help because others thought I needed to go. Very quickly I realised I had to want to help myself or it would not work out. Being sexually abused knocked all the motivation out of me that I ever had. I really did not see the point of anything, including living. To think in terms of goals or aspirations – these were not part of my thinking.'

- If I had five pounds for everyone who has said to me, 'there's no point', I would be very rich, as that is one of the commonest feelings abused people report. Some readers could probably write on this subject for me. Someone who feels hopeless is saying, 'I am at the end of myself, there is nowhere to go but down, life will never improve.' Despair can feel like depression that has set like concrete.

- A person may struggle physically, emotionally and spiritually, at the same time as having problems with relationships, with trust, confidence and security, or with how they view their own sexuality. Such a combination of factors can lead to a deep sense of hopelessness. In such circumstances people might make unhelpful decisions or be indecisive; their choices might be made for defensive or self-protective reasons. All this tends to be particularly true of people who have been sexually abused.

- Possible roots of despair can include abuse itself, not being listened to and unresolved emotional pain.

- Hopelessness can come into a person's life because of the long-term nature of the damage done by abuse. It is understandable that someone who has suffered abuse might experience despair, and feel that there is no hope for getting better. It can be easier to believe that there is no longer hope for change than to wonder how the uphill climb out of despair can be tackled.

- Looking inward and focusing on the problem rather than on possible answers is a common cause of a continuing sense of hopelessness. Choosing to look outwards can help to break the sense of desperation and pessimism that comes along with hopelessness. Shifting one's focus from inward emotional turmoil onto another person or another situation by doing something practical can be very helpful. Ways forward might include establishing a worthwhile routine with events that are enjoyable but not too demanding, taking up a new hobby, or seeking to serve others, perhaps in voluntary work. Trusting God to pour in hope to replace the hopelessness is something many of my clients have proved to be effective, enabling them to take the first hesitant steps forward.

Identity crisis

'What a feeling I have of not being alive! There is a void. I don't know who I am and am not sure I want to know. In fact, I feel I have got stuck at the age I was when I was traumatised by abuse, when I was only twelve. My mind is blank, with no real sense of anything, either past, present or future. I can recognise an emptiness.'

- To have an identity is to be content as the person you are for the most part. An identity crisis is a time when an individual experiences or senses a breakdown of identity. Sexual abuse can have a particularly damaging effect on a person's sense of identity, robbing a person of the ability to think or feel for him or herself. Sometimes there can be a preference to be someone else and a denial of one's own thoughts and opinions, because that is what the abuser has insisted on for so long.

- A question we ask clients regularly is, 'in whom or what do you find your identity?' The answer to this question often reveals what or who is of greatest importance to the person. One client responded, 'When I heard myself say that my identity was in my CD collection, I realised, sadly, that I was running away from the real issues in my life. Having been sexually, physically and emotionally abused, I hid in my music. I chose to destroy my CDs and a major amount of emotion hit me which I was then able to face head on and deal with bit by bit.'

- How we see ourself often determines how we cope emotionally and how we relate to others. Rebuilding personal identity can be a lengthy process, but it is at the heart of real healing. There is a need to move on from waiting on someone else to tell us who we are and to learn that we are a person in our own right. A useful strategy is to write down a few positive statements about who you are, not necessarily what you do. This list will help to shape and form a person's identity and correct wrong beliefs about self, which were brought about by abuse.

- Knowing they belong to God and are his children has released many people into discovering their own identity. In other words, God created us to be individuals with a separate and distinctive identity or personality. A healthy sense of identity grows as a person sees the damage of the past repaired, makes his (or her) own decisions that are right for him, and refuses to allow himself to be controlled by others. Establishing good boundaries is essential (see chapter 5). See also chapter 4 for more on identity and self-image.

Loneliness

'My husband's sexual violence towards me is like a private prison. He is well thought of in the community, so I dare not say anything about how he is at home. I am, therefore, isolated and feel set apart from humanity. This aloneness is destructive for me, as I feel so lost and desolate.'

- Loneliness, for an abused person, is often experienced as a sense of isolation, of being misunderstood, of being the only one who ever suffered in this way, a lack of meaningful connection with others.

- For most people, even if they have been abused, there is still a desire of some sort to relate significantly with other people. That's the way God intended us to be when he made us (Eccles. 4:9-12). When these connections with other human beings are lacking or break down, people suffer, and loneliness is a by-product. It should be noted that loneliness is not solitude; that is an experience of enjoying one's own company as an active choice. Most people need experiences of solitude and personal space as well as interaction with other people, some more than others.

- Healthy connections with people and with God help to resolve loneliness. Connectedness can be defined as the sense of self in relation to others. We have been created to have a vital connection with God himself and also with other people. Human beings are mostly highly sociable and interdependent. We are meant to live in communities and relate significantly to others.

- It would be best to seek out non-threatening involvement with people on a fairly surface level to begin with, in a context where there is little risk involved. Going to the cinema, a further education class or swimming, where other people are around but there is little expectation

76

of involvement or communication, has helped others. Dog walking, which may seem a solitary pastime, can lead to conversations with other dog lovers. Attending church may help to provide a sense of family and real friendships. Gradually, over time, a deeper sense of connection or interdependence may develop. See further chapter 5.

Loss, see *Grief.*

Powerlessness

'The vulnerability I have always felt in my life is rooted in the powerlessness of being abused when it was entirely against my will. This has left me with the strong idea that I am incapable of making choices, which in turn makes me act like I have no power. Counselling has helped me to see that I can make good choices and I have learned to say no.'

- Powerlessness comes about when someone else takes control in a person's life without permission. The abused person feels dominated by the abuser and trapped by the inability to choose what happens. This brings with it feelings of incapacity and having a total lack of emotional strength.
- The abused person may become powerless and weak, causing them to be emotionally debilitated and even paralysed, leading to feelings of inadequacy and helplessness. This sense of powerlessness does not seem to stop when the abuse stops. It can go on affecting someone until it is specifically addressed.
- For someone who is abused as a child, the opportunity to make choices seems to be unrealistic. Such a child

feels, and often is, powerless to prevent or stop the abuse. However, anyone who has been abused as a child needs to realise that as an adult there is no longer any need to be intimidated by the control or domination of an abuser. Even as an adult looking back on abuse, it can be tough to admit that powerlessness to stop the abuser.

- Not every relationship is unhealthy and controlling. People need to seek out quality relationships where they can be themselves. Counselling may help to break any ongoing power issues with the abuser and look at how this power can be completely broken. Once that is done, powerlessness has a lot less to feed on. The goal is to move on to empowerment that will change the course of life in the future. See also chapter 5 on re-building trust with others.

Rejection

'In all my relationships, especially with people I am close to, I am just waiting for them to reject me. This only began when I was abused, but it is now how I genuinely feel. I presume rejection and I fear it, so much so, that I induce it to save waiting. My behaviour is erratic and confrontational as a result. I say to myself that nobody wants me or likes me.'

'It is terrible to admit, but this rejection was the hardest thing for me to deal with because it was so deep. Obviously my abuser planted the rejection deep within me. It has taken quite a lot of emotional surgery to get to the bottom of it, but now I am free of it I feel like an entirely new person. I have a new ability to trust people and I have developed one special friendship and the guy has neither abused me nor rejected me. This is a first. He knows about what has happened to me and he is angry about it. His anger released me by helping me to see that I was right to be mad at what my abuser did to me. The physical scars healed quite quickly but I am determined that through time all the other scars will go as well.'

- Most abused people feel rejection, since abuse is such an offensive, demeaning and 'knock-back' experience. It challenges the person to their very core. In essence abuse is the rejection of a person by denying him or her personal boundaries and choices as to what happens to his or her body. The abuser, who effectively rejected the person and his or her beliefs about what should happen between two people, cast any opinions or morals aside.
- Sexual abuse is a rejecting experience, with a great robbery of confidence, security and trust. Suffering from rejection can lead to an expectation that rejection will always be part of life and is therefore inevitable.
- The deep-down hurt and reasons for past rejection ought to be addressed and healed so that present rejection and fear of future rejection can be tackled before it becomes intolerable. Knowing the unconditional acceptance and love of God can be an effective antidote to rejection.

Self-harm

'I felt so bad that I wanted to hurt myself; it helps me to numb the pain in my heart. My arms are all scarred and the doctors have tried to stop me from doing this by medicating me.'

- Many people indulge in behaviour that is harmful to their own personhood. The trauma of abuse can trigger this kind of self-harming behaviour. Often self-harming is repetitive, impulsive and can become compulsive, with vulnerability and the need to be in control as motivating factors. Sometimes an abused person feels a desire for physical pain to detract from the internal emotional pain, or as a punishment of some kind. This is a subconscious drive for the most part, and is not normally an attempt to end life. It is possible to display self-harming behaviour without having any sense of self-hatred.

- Pain can be inflicted in a variety of ways, including cutting with a knife, burning, hitting, bruising, breaking bones, excessive hair pulling, scratching and mutilation. It may show itself in more minor ways, such as pinching or digging the nails in, although such practices leave no visible damage. The feelings that provoke self-harm can be intense and inwardly directed, leading to actions that are a way of expressing in a tangible way the pain of the heart, which the person finds impossible to express in any other way. It can also be part of disassociation, where a person's personality fragments into various parts. One part of the person may be destructive and have a desire to harm himself or herself. Disassociation is mentioned in chapter 2.

- To deal with self-harm it is necessary to find the root cause of this behaviour and to change the person's underlying assumptions about himself or herself from negative and harmful ones to healthy ones. For example, a client of ours believed she was unlovable. Once she was able to alter that belief, she did not feel the same need to harm herself. She began to love herself as well as to receive love from people and God.

- Changing one's routine to involve other people and to have goals for each day can help to break the habit of self-harming. Discouraging loneliness and avoiding occupations where there is little stimulation or involvement with other people helps too.

Shame

'I can hardly go into public places because shame rises to the front of my mind. I feel other people will see what happened to me just by the look on my face. I am virtually a prisoner in my own home.'

'With determination I decided to talk to my counsellor about the crushing shame I felt most days. It was especially bad because I felt it wasn't manly to feel this way – it doubled my shame. My counsellor wonderfully understood that I would feel this and helped me to deal with it by showing me whose shame it was. Also I discovered that Jesus died to deal with this shame and all my other symptoms. As I handed them over to him bit by bit, he took the sting out of each one. Now, at family occasions, when I have to meet my unrepentant abuser, I have learned not to be cowed in any way. This feels like freedom and feels good. There is a real sense that I have moved forward and I am ready now to deal with the next thing that crops up.'

- Shame is a painful emotion resulting from an awareness of having been involved in something that is wrong, unworthy, degrading or disgraceful. The consequences of shame can be secrecy, isolation, alienation, depression and self-hatred. Powerlessness, fear and the shock of abuse can all contribute to a sense of shame. Shame is often number one on the list of emotions commonly felt after abuse.
- There can be a desire to hide and take cover. Shame would say, 'There is something wrong with me.' In actual fact, the abuser's shame has been imposed on the recipient of

abuse, and what should be said is, 'There is something wrong with my abuser.' Every abuser creates shame in the person they hurt; it is part of the wounding.

- To deal with shame there has to be an acknowledgement that the shame belongs to the abuser not to the abused person. Continuing to own shame is to give the abuser ongoing power. The good news is that emotional wounds can be healed and shame can be a thing of the past. Apart from dealing with the emotional aspect of shame, there are practical steps that can be taken to help someone cope in social situations. Choosing comfortable clothes to wear, and consciously adopting a confident outward posture, with head held high, can help to cut through that sense of shame.

Suicidal thoughts

'My father interfered with me and I have felt there was no point in going on with life. My teachers at school and my mum have been brilliant and now I am trying to talk to them when I feel bad. It helps a lot.' It was a serious suicide attempt that brought this particular case of abuse to light.

- Suicide is a tragic and potentially preventable issue that is rarely discussed; yet many people attempt suicide. Abused people look for ways out of their emotional pain, and if they feel it has become unmanageable, suicide can be considered an option. These thoughts come alongside guilt, shame, hopelessness, depression and despair. The first thought of suicide can seem shocking to the person, but if allowed to take root, can begin to feel tempting.
- Suicide is seen as a solution to a problem and a way to end pain. The risk of committing suicide is increased if

this thought is regular and if a plan to carry it out has been made.

- If such thoughts are to be altered, life needs to be regarded as an option that can be actively and consciously chosen. Saying 'yes' to life is the best way to counteract the thought of suicide and is possible through a series of little decisions made over time. Usually choosing life is no mean feat, and it requires a lot of effort to continue with that choice. People who have suicidal thoughts need a lot of help to get hold of the belief that life is worth living, and should actively seek help and support. Friends, relatives and health professionals should take every suicide threat seriously.

- If you are feeling suicidal as you read, help should be sought from any professional in your life, your doctor, counsellor or whoever. Try and share what you are feeling with someone you trust. Help is available. You can get better. I would encourage you to keep on trying and not give up. It is just a matter of finding the right help for you. The following helplines can help by offering a listening ear, support and counselling. The Samaritans are on 08457 90 90 90 and have a website www. samaritans.org. Crossline is a Christian telephone helpline and is on 01482 620 820 and at www.crossline. org.uk. The Edinburgh Crossline telephone number is 0845 658 0045.[3]

Trust, (lack of), see chapter 5

Unforgiveness
- Unforgiveness is very common among people who have suffered at the hands of an abuser. In the context of this

---

3. For international contact details see the appendix.

book unforgiveness is taken to mean that there is no willingness to forgive the abuser for the abuse suffered and all its implications. To remain in unforgiveness causes emotional pain and turmoil for the person who has been wronged, but hasty forgiveness is not an option either; it needs to be reasoned and willingly given. Premature forgiveness can be another form of denial. It is often difficult for people to grasp that forgiveness is a choice and not a feeling, although feelings do catch up after choosing to forgive. Forgiving someone means that a choice is made to pardon the abuser.

- Forgiveness is an act of will, a decision that is possible even when feelings are still raw. Inevitably, forgiveness will be a process and should be dealt with as the need for it comes to light. Approaching the issue of forgiveness with someone who has been abused requires great sensitivity and wisdom, and should only be suggested after careful consideration of where the individual is in his or her healing process. It is not a topic to be approached lightly or used as a surface plaster over an open wound. In the long run however, there are great benefits in forgiving others as it lifts an emotional burden.

- Forgiveness is only possible in the light of a moral judgment, that is, when the abused person recognises that the abuser is clearly in the wrong and to blame for the abuse.

- It is good to choose to forgive, whether or not the abuser is asking for forgiveness by admitting guilt, so that the abused person can put the past behind him or her. However, forgiving an abuser does not release him or her from the need to repent of the sin of abusing; what that person did was not, and never will be, acceptable either to society or to God.

- When we find forgiveness it is a mark of the character of God, not something God owes us or that we deserve. In the same way, the abuser does not deserve forgiveness, but may find it if he truly repents. To truly forgive involves not talking about the hurt of the offence except in order to deal with the next layer of healing, and not dwelling on the offence. See also forgiveness under 'the choice of forgiveness' in chapter 6.

'It was a very long time before I forgave my two abusers. Forgiveness was a somewhat alien subject to me and I had not really understood that in order to get free from the effects of my abuse I had to move from a place of unforgiveness to a place of forgiveness. Following that route changed my life completely.'

'My daddy abused me. It was a major challenge to consider forgiving him, given that he had harmed me so deeply. I had to clearly blame him for the abuse. Then I chose to forgive him. Only afterwards could I begin to quantify the robbery of being in unforgiveness for years. It absolutely stunted my growth as a person and kept me tied to my painful past.'

Worthlessness see chapter 4.

CHAPTER 4

MOVING ON

Hope for healing

There is a commonly held notion that recovery after sexual abuse is unlikely. My view, after twenty years of counselling, is entirely different. Painful experiences can be transformed. Although the symptoms that come from being abused can feel overwhelming, it is vital to know that there is hope for healing. One of the reasons I have written this book is to reach out to people I may never meet to stress that there is life beyond sexual abuse, a life beyond all the implications and symptoms which can accompany that abuse.

Usually hope has to come from outside, because there is little hope left on the inside to work with. Help can be sought from family, friends, professionals or pastoral workers. In my experience of counselling those broken by sexual abuse, it is unusual for a person to deal with all the torn emotions and anguish which sexual abuse so often leaves behind without help of some kind. People often need compassionate and patient support in order to find the strength required to deal with their damaged innermost feelings and emotions. It is the job of a counsellor to help inspire hope as the counselling process proceeds, based on their experience of seeing other hurting people find hope and healing. Hope can also grow through understanding that there is a God who cares and has the power and will to help.

Timing

Everyone needs to be aware of what is true about their own life, whether or not they have been abused. It is always hard work to face uncomfortable truths, and it takes a great deal of courage. Facing the truth is often a matter of timing, and involves the breaking of old thought patterns.

In counselling it is essential to go at the person's own pace and to exercise patience. If denial has been a part of someone's life for a long time, it can be a tremendous struggle to face up to the truth of what happened. There is often a stage when someone discovers or gradually realises that abuse has taken place. When counselling, however, I try to take this 'revelation stage' very slowly with people because of the extreme difficulty some people experience in this area. It is no surprise that facing emotional pain is a costly business, and what this does to a person who is willing to walk this road should never be underestimated. However such a 'revelation' may be needed before abused people can be sure that abuse was a genuine part of their experience. Only when a person is certain about this can real counselling and healing begin.

Henry slowly became aware that healing was a possibility for him. That hope, and a belief that things could change, gave him the motivation to face up to his abuse. Henry comments:

> It was like a dawning in my mind that I really had been sexually abused. I guess it took me a few years to understand that boys and men can be harmed in this way and that help was available for me. The real motivation for me in seeking help was my belief that I would be happier if I could deal with some of my symptoms.

If someone is struggling to face up to painful realities, it may be helpful to offer the reassurance that in coming out of denial into truth there is not necessarily a need to re-experience past hurts in order to be made whole. However, these past hurts do need to be recognised and dealt with. Facing the past and all its traumas will include dealing with emotional pain that is hidden under a cloak of unreality, but in the long run this process will bring increased peace. No matter what age a person is when they start looking for help, all the hurts of childhood can be addressed, and the person can move towards some kind of resolution. By resolution I mean that there will be a significant lessening of symptoms, and hopefully an ability to draw a line under the past. Even if sexual abuse happened long ago, all the symptoms can be dealt with, bit by bit, once a person is ready to deal with them. The future will certainly look brighter once emotional pain is resolved.

It takes a lot of emotional energy to deny the truth and to sustain that position. The indecision of holding opposing opinions about whether or not abuse happened is also draining. Nevertheless, it needs to be recognised that some people prefer to remain in the false security of their problems, and lack the motivation to embark on a process of healing and change, because staying where they are can seem a 'safe place' for them. Often, however, the issue is one of timing, not willingness or unwillingness. Carers and counsellors need to exercise discernment, and ask the right questions: for instance, 'does this person want help and is he or she ready for it?' Sometimes the carer is more anxious than the abused person to find help. I have the greatest compassion for people who say they are not yet able to look at the pain they are experiencing within themselves. For this reason, as a friend, relative or counsellor, it is important to recognise when someone is not yet ready to face reality.

I was once called into a situation in which two counsellors were trying to help a lady who had suffered from abuse. When I arrived in the room, the lady was sitting on the floor and looked like a scared cat. The two counsellors were standing over her, which struck me as intimidating. I immediately got down on to the floor near her, but not so near as to intrude on her personal space. I looked at her and said, 'It's not safe for you here, is it?' She shook her head and began to weep with relief that her silent scream had been heard. The two counsellors had been so keen to follow their own agenda, whatever that was, that they had not recognised that the lady had had more than enough that day. She was very distressed, and clearly needed tender loving care, not confrontation about a subject that was altogether too difficult for her at that stage. The end of this story is a happy one. When this lady got more appropriate help, with people she felt were safe for her to relate to and share with, she was able to deal with her past hurts.

It takes phenomenal courage to face up to such painful realities. Over the years I have had the privilege of walking alongside many of these brave individuals and sharing in their transformation. Before they can begin to deal with that pain, however, abused people have to want to let denial go and have to feel that they need to do so. If the people trying to help the abused person, whether friends, relatives or counsellors, knew the pain behind the person's difficulties, they might not be so keen to disturb old wounds, especially when they might not be equipped to help that person cope with the issues raised. Sadly, in my work, I have regularly had to pick up the pieces of well-meaning friends or counsellors who had 'diagnosed' the problem and then left the person with a superficial answer which neither reduced the pain, nor made any real attempt to help them map out a route to healing. One counsellor I knew ran into difficulties when he tried to get a lady to forgive her abuser. This process was not working at all for his client, who eventually agreed that I should be called in to try to resolve the situation. Within a short space of time it became abundantly clear that this lady was not even sure that she had been abused. I agreed with the client that she was unable to proceed until she was sure, and she went on her way knowing that if she became sure of what had happened to her, there were things she could do to resolve the symptoms she was suffering. I regarded this lady as being at what I call 'the revelation stage'. In other words, she was just becoming aware of the fact that she had been abused and was still at the early stages of remembering what had happened. The counsellor had been giving a textbook answer too early in the proceedings. It is never appropriate to embark on healing before the client is sure of what happened to them as that might create yet another abusive situation in which the client is put into a passive role whilst others decide what he (or she) should do.

Trusting a counsellor

Once a person is ready to start facing past hurts, or at least ready to consider the possibility of doing so, the idea of having counselling may arise. Knowing what to expect when going to see a counsellor for the first time can do much to reassure people and persuade them to give counselling a try. Going into the unknown can be very intimidating, particularly when someone is in an emotionally vulnerable state, and when the issues to be discussed are so painful and private. Unburdening to a total stranger is very often something people find exceptionally hard, especially people who have been sexually abused. For that reason, just crossing the threshold can be a tremendous achievement, and a good counsellor will be aware of that. I will never forget a lady, whom I will call Dawn, who came for counselling and sat at the door constantly watching that her exit was clear. Dawn had been in a professional relationship with a person who raped her in terrifying and unexpected circumstances. She had developed a real mistrust of all authority figures as a result. Just coming through the door of a counsellor's office represented great cost on her part. For Dawn's second visit, she was much happier to have someone else sitting in the room whilst she was counselled. She felt I would not then take advantage of her, and she felt safer and more secure. Very slowly, she doubted our motives less and less and began to trust us. In facing her vulnerability, Dawn discovered that counselling became a place of healing and not a place to experience further pain.

Any number of barriers can prevent people from seeking counselling help. Abused people may feel there is no point to counselling, or that they are not worthy of help, or the fear of exposing raw emotions is too risky. Some may have had unfortunate experiences of poor counselling. Good counsellors are often hard to locate and then might have a waiting list. It is best to get on to a waiting list as soon as it is thought that counselling might help. Personal recommendation of a good counsellor is helpful. Counsellors are listed in the yellow pages and there are associations for counsellors which provide guidance.[1]

So what can someone expect to happen on a first visit to a counsellor? It is our practice to conduct a first counselling

---

1. Christian counsellors often register with the Association of Christian Counselling www.acc-uk.org. Postal address: The Association of Christian Counsellors, 29 Momus Boulevard, Coventry, CV2 5NA, England. Tel. 0845 124 9569. Another professional agency is the British Association of Counsellors and Psychotherapy, www.bacp.co.uk. Postal address: BACP House, 35-37 Albert Street, Rugby, Warwickshire, CV21 2SG. Tel. 0870 443 5252, email: bacp@bacp.co.uk. The agency I founded is Dove Christian Counselling, Postal address: 110 St. James Road, Glasgow, G4 0PS Tel. 0141 552 5120, email info@dove.uk.net. For international contact details see the appendix.

appointment without there being any obligation to return or embark on a series of counselling interviews. If the client is able to talk about the issues and difficulties they are experiencing in their lives during the first visit, we set out possible ways of dealing with these issues in future sessions, explain what might be involved, what some of the landmarks might be and what might be achieved. Sometimes people prefer to go away and think about whether or not they want to commit to counselling. We always try to make a person feel as relaxed as possible, knowing that a visit to a counsellor can be a little nerve wracking initially. Many clients have reported to us that although difficult emotions were being looked at in subsequent sessions, the first visit was the most testing. After that a relationship of trust grew and counselling could even be enjoyable.

I hope that clients feel in control of what is discussed and able to say as much or as little as they wish. It should be an opportunity for the person to get to know the counsellor, and decide whether to take it any further. Since emotional scars and past hurts are the two main reasons why abused people seek counselling, it can be understandably difficult for them to trust anyone. One of the aims of counselling is to build a trust relationship with a client. Often, when people first come, it is easier for them to talk about their circumstances than share their feelings or talk about the actual abuse they have experienced. In a first interview, clients can feel greatly helped simply because they have been listened to. Although nothing has changed and the deep issues have not yet been addressed, there can be a real sense of relief that they have found somewhere where understanding, empathy and quality time is given. No real counselling may take place at this stage, but trust between client and counsellor has begun to be established.

For the most part, a diagnostic first interview usually begins with more surface material and goes into the subjects more deeply as and when the client feels able. The sharing of one's heart does not always come easily and considerable skill is required to put the client at ease. Once the issues are clear (and that may take several appointments), they have to be worked through to some kind of satisfactory conclusion. I remember one client who was unable to let us get near the issues surrounding abuse. When we were able to show her that we could be trusted by sorting out an apparently minor issue, she chose to trust us with the deeper and more challenging problems. Although ultimately the roots or origins of the problems have to be addressed, in the initial stages of getting help with a counsellor it can be invaluable to deal with some of the more surface or obvious issues. This allows a clearing up of circumstances and damaged relationships in a way that allows for personal growth.

Subsequent sessions are linked by a variety of possible tasks that allow a client to use the time between sessions to think through some of the issues raised in counselling. This link–work is always agreed with the person involved. For example, Felicity was struggling to pin down what her abuser had actually done to her. Having discussed the possibilities at one session, she had a week to think before we met again, and by then she was more ready to face the issues she had raised. Another week she was asked to look at her own positive attributes, and came back the following week with a blank sheet. That had been altogether too hard for her. Felicity was staggered that over a full week she could not think up one positive thing to say about herself. This motivated her to examine why this was the case. By the time Felicity ended counselling her self-esteem was much healthier.

When counselling a couple, it is often helpful to use communication or listening exercises. The tasks get more involved as time goes on. One lady thought in pictures, so she would come each week with a drawing or a painting to describe how she felt through the week. Others have written poetry. It is common to ask people to keep an emotional diary where they record their feelings. This is not for the counsellor to read, but to help the client to get in touch with his or her emotions. Abused people sometimes find it helpful to write a letter to their abuser which expresses how they really feel, although usually we would not recommend sending it.

Trusting takes time, and it is vital that a client is allowed to set the pace and be comfortable with the proposed agenda. Clients often give clues as to how best they may be helped. For instance, one person might always keep referring back to a person who was obviously significant in her (or his) life. This can be an indication that the client has a desire to look at the influence this person has had in their particular circumstances. At any stage in counselling a person can decide that he or she no longer wants to continue with the agreed work. This is always the person's choice. If there is any feeling of discomfort or unhappiness in the counselling process, it can be voiced at any time.

There is no set period of time for recovery from abuse. The timescale and route to wholeness is different for every individual, so no two people will be counselled in the same way. I often outline the sort of route healing might take in a first interview, because although not all the issues are going to be worked through immediately, the client is often reassured by knowing the ground that will have to be covered. It may also help someone trapped in despair and hopelessness to understand that healing is a process, and that there really is hope that change can take place. Much will depend on how the client feels and the particular circumstances of his or her situation. The willingness to face painful emotions, to trust the counsellor and the support available for that person outside counselling, will all have a role in determining the process and timescale of healing. Not everyone achieves total healing, and some people turn back, for different reasons, even after coming for counselling for some time. However, the majority of those I have sought to help over the years have made significant progress, and feel that their lives are better now than they were before they came for counselling.

One of the hallmarks of the counselling I have practised over the years is that most work has been done with two counsellors present (with the client's consent), even if one of them was in training and had a far less vocal role. This has worked for a variety of reasons. People seem to get healed more quickly, have less of a tendency to become dependent, and can be supported and understood by more than one counsellor. It also facilitates the development of trust, as the client knows that a witness is always present, offering a sense of protection in what can feel like a vulnerable situation. I never counsel someone of the opposite sex alone. If this were unacceptable to the person, then he would have to seek counselling elsewhere.

People move towards wholeness in a variety of ways because every individual is unique, with their own background, upbringing, temperament, expectations and life experiences. There is no one method or approach that will work every time for every situation.

Human dignity

One of the keys to living on the other side of abuse and rising above the symptoms is to gain a fresh understanding of one's value and worth. Human dignity stems from the fact that all human beings have the capacity for moral choice, which is not shared by any other species on earth. All human beings are born equal in dignity and rights, and these concepts form an integral part of our humanity. Acknowledging and enhancing the inherent dignity of every individual, and respecting personal and cultural diversity is the best way to ensure that people feel valued in their own right. I and many others would agree with biblical teaching, which is that all of humanity is worthy of honour and respect because human beings have been created in the image of God and are thus all of equal value. God does not judge a person's value by actions or lifestyle. People are of infinite value to God, and quality of life is diminished when a person is not valued and treated with dignity and respect. Sexual abusers totally disregard the dignity of the person they choose to abuse, and this is the source of a great deal of emotional pain.

Seeing life, the past, pain and worth from God's perspective rather than their own can be a very effective way for people to begin the process of healing. Knowing that they are of eternal worth to God often enables people to recover their sense of who they really are and to see that their own thoughts and opinions are valid. The Bible teaches that human beings bear the image of God; they are rational, thinking beings with moral responsibility for their actions, created not just with the ability to have a relationship with God, but for that very purpose. The fact that Jesus Christ experienced life on earth as a human being reinforces the Bible's teaching that everyone is of infinite worth in God's eyes. Indeed, so much does God love us, that he allowed his only Son, Jesus, to endure not only the physical agony of flogging and crucifixion, but also the inner torment of mockery, humiliation, rejection and separation from God his Father. For Christians, the fact that Jesus went all the way to death on the cross, so that all grief and sorrow could be dealt with by his sacrifice, means that he knows all about suffering from his personal experience whilst on earth. When people admit that they cannot deal with the consequences of sexual abuse on their own, and ask for God's help, they come to a God who is both willing and able to come into people's lives, bringing freedom and release.

Self-image

It is often the case that an abused person has a poor self-image and does not see himself or herself as someone with a real identity, a person in his or her own right, with opinions, dislikes and preferences. The sexually abused person often feels labelled by his or her broken identity or poor self-image. Labels given in childhood by hurtful words spoken, or because of circumstances, can carry over into adult life in a person's perception of who he or she is, continuing to cause further pain, shame or brokenness. I remember Carol, who was repeatedly told by her abuser that 'no man would ever have her'. This negative talk along with abuse made Carol feel she would never marry and that she was different from all her peers. Carol grew up into adulthood having severe difficulties with relationships. Her self-esteem was at a low ebb and she worried constantly about her future.

To move towards healing is to embrace the idea of moving on from the label 'sexually abused' and to walk free of the trauma and the resulting symptoms. Everyone needs to have a sense of identity or personal worth, knowing who they are as individuals rather than as 'abuse sufferers' or 'survivors'. In other words, to be free to be a person who is no longer identified by the pain of the past, but who has a healthy self-image. For Christians, identity is shaped and formed by the recognition that God in Jesus accepts them as they are, and that they can continue to walk daily with him. God's image of us as humans has a great bearing on our own understanding of who we are as persons. His understanding of us and his view of our importance as individuals in his overall plan for the world is fundamental to our acceptance of ourselves. In other words, if our creator underlines our worth and value, then we should learn to do the same.

Traumatic events like abuse can interfere with the developing sense of personal worth and self-image. Most people have a desire to develop their potential, but an abused person may be unaware of such a desire. It may be that this desire has never come to the surface or been accessed. It is not uncommon for abused people to look to other people to tell them who they are. Even counsellors can sometimes be expected to tell a client how to feel, what to do and who they are. It is neither right nor possible for a counsellor to perform this role.

For some, perfectionism becomes a way of compensating for a lack of identity and poor self-image. Perfectionism is the uncompromising pursuit of excellence. When Sally's world toppled, she believed that there would be no recovery. For a long time she had known that she had been abused, but was devastated when another girl took the same abuser to court. She was called as a witness but could not cope with appearing upset in public, seeing her abuser again or any other aspect of her own pain that might have come up during the court case. No one would have known that Sally had been abused. She was in a good job, married to a man who had no idea about her being abused. Her 'perfect' world crumbled. The recovery started when Sally was able to face the fact that life was not perfect and that her perfectionism was a cover or defence to stop her facing the pain that was most definitely within her.

Whilst being abused there can be an attempt to perform perfectly for the abuser. Unfortunately this rarely reduces either the duration or violence of the episode. If trying to be perfect or good becomes habitual, it can affect every part of a person's life. It can also be a mask to cover the pain that comes with abuse. Moving towards healing means a person is able to be honest with himself or herself in regard to faults and mistakes and accept that failure is not the end of the world.

Part of the healing process is for the abused person to move towards feeling good about self, to be happy inside, to achieve inner contentment and peace. If there is a growing sense of worth being formed, there will be an ever-increasing knowledge of being a real person and greater emotional security. Lack of self-worth can be a particular issue because no choice was given about being abused. There is often a sense of powerlessness. This directly feeds into abused people feeling that what they have said is of no importance or value, because in the past they were regularly ignored. Therefore, abused people often feel that they, as well as their words, are viewed as neither important nor valuable. Such people often report feelings of non-being, or being a non-person.

A healthy self-image

Self-acceptance is a belief in one's personal worth and value. To accept himself or herself is one of the greatest challenges to be faced by the abused person. Those who are emotionally damaged through sexual abuse should be encouraged, when they are ready, to address the distorted beliefs they have developed about themselves over time. The abused person needs to know his worth and value. This is a fundamental belief for anyone if they are to have a healthy self-image. As we have already seen, God made human beings in his own image, and the consequence of this is that everyone should respect himself or herself and other people. Equally, everyone should be able to expect to be treated with respect by others.

Sadly, a lack of self-acceptance and low self-esteem is increasingly common these days, but is particularly prevalent among those who have suffered sexual abuse. To love oneself does not come naturally to the abused person. To see someone beginning to believe in himself or herself is a great joy for me as a counsellor. I remember one young man, whom I will call

George, who was robbed of any sense of personal worth because of the treatment he suffered at the hands of an abuser. George thought and acted as if he was entirely unlovable. He disliked himself intensely and never let anyone get close to him. It was clear he wanted good relationships, but his stumbling-block was a deeply held belief that he was unlovable. For years George put up barriers between himself and other people. Once he began to love himself, George was able to take on board other people's love for him. He is now in a happy marriage, and together George and his wife trust God in their day-to-day living. This would never have been an option for him had he not dealt radically with his self-hatred. He did this by working at knocking down each barrier he had unknowingly erected, one by one. One of George's barriers meant he could not freely cope with the company of women or even speaking to them. His first step towards recovery was to speak to the cashier at the supermarket. Usually he lowered his head and made an indecipherable grunt instead of sharing superficial pleasantries. He was thrilled when he kept his head high and said 'thank you'. The next plan was to speak to the lady librarian and ask for a book, and that worked well too. More risk was taken when George asked someone to go out for coffee with him. The lady was very pleased to go out with him and understood when he felt twenty minutes was enough! Nowadays, George is embarrassed to think he had to take such small steps initially, but he has no regrets. The lady in question was patient and, in fact, is now his wife. I guess he learned a lot about loving himself and loving others!

Henry writes about his experience of moving towards self-acceptance:

> I have come to a place of self-acceptance, which I never thought was possible. I can look in the mirror, smile at myself and say, 'God did a good job when he made me!' It wasn't always this

way. I had an extreme tendency to look inward, not helped by perpetual studying. My worth and identity would come from excelling in my studies. The standard of perfection I expected of myself nearly crushed my 'self' and my spirituality. All I could think of was spending hour after hour studying – and even then I wasn't satisfied. I was pursuing the wrong goal. My value and worth are not about what I do or what I can achieve, but about who I am in Jesus.

Being busy consumed me and life was passing me by. I had no way of stopping the cycle until I realised the foolishness of my lifestyle. God has done a work of healing which has freed me to have a healthier self-image. Nowadays I can actually rest and I can sit and be still. I am able to acknowledge God's presence more as a reality. I put far more importance now on God's perspective and have given up navel gazing as a waste of good time and energy. Yes, I am an okay chap. I've stopped arguing with God about the way he made me. He saw what he had made and it was good. He knows best. I am uniquely put together and God made a pretty good job of me. Self-acceptance is growing in me but I am not proud per se. I have had to learn where my dependence lies, namely in the One who created me. Agreeing that I am okay does not indicate that I have arrived, but rather that God is in the process of healing me. I also used to compare myself to other men all the time. That was a product of my insecurity.

As Henry helpfully illustrates, not only does a negative view of self consume a lot of energy, but it also robs the abused person of peace. Low self-esteem and the burden of busyness are tyrannies of our modern society. Henry has come right through on some of these issues. He is a humble man who has grasped that true masculinity for him is not about being macho or about being performance-orientated. He is now experiencing life in a more meaningful way than ever before.[2]

2. There is more about damaged sexuality in chapter 7.

For someone suffering the effects of abuse, I would say it is actually more painful to remain in emotional pain and turmoil than to move forward with help, from whatever source. Then there can be increased healing of insecurities and hopefully a more positive self-image. Some of my clients, who have come into an understanding of God's acceptance of who they are, have found they can begin to move more easily into self-acceptance. Other clients have preferred to work on their issues without God's help. Olive is one of these:

> It was with some anxiety that I went to a Christian counselling agency for help with abuse issues, but they were the only people who were recommended. I was never impressed with Christian thinking. However, the Christians I met helped me within my own framework. They were able to cope professionally and skillfully with my atheism and my desire to deal with my symptoms. I am considerably better in myself and in my relationships, although I still don't believe in God. My estimation of myself has risen from zilch to reasonable, and I continue to work on it.

Developing a healthier self-image is a vital part of starting on the road to recovery, as people like George, Henry and Olive have discovered. It may take a considerable amount of time and effort for someone to unlearn old thought patterns and beliefs, and to choose consistently and consciously to move on from the past into a brighter future, but it is possible. Increasing self-acceptance should bring with it a greater sense of inner peace and an ability to cope better with the challenges of life. Rebuilding trust has a vital part to play in healing, and the next two chapters explore this topic in greater depth.

CHAPTER 5

REBUILDING TRUST VERTICALLY

What is trust?
The reader may be reflecting that the ability to put any of the advice of the previous chapters into practice will depend ultimately on a person's willingness to trust – whether that be trusting the author, other people, one's self or God. As was mentioned in the last chapter, the whole issue of trust is something that can cause difficulties in the life of someone who has been sexually abused.

According to the Oxford Dictionary, trust is 'a firm belief in the reliability or truth or strength ... of a person ...' It is voluntarily depending upon someone else for some particular reason. Trust is essential for living, because interaction is not possible without it; the world would be an impossible place if nobody trusted anyone else. In a very real sense, each of us has to trust every day, whether it is the doctor, the post office or a friend. Babies are absolutely trusting of those who are around them, but sadly that innocent trust of childhood is often replaced by mistrust and suspicion as life goes on. Painful experiences can rob people of the willingness and sometimes the ability to trust others, especially when an important relationship is involved. The more important the relationship, the more vital is the need to trust. For example, a large amount of trust is required in a marriage. Similarly, a business partnership cannot function well without trust between the partners. Such trust is not usually a one-off act, but rather a process of little choices and decisions that ultimately constitute trust. Trust is always a process that has to be given time to develop.

Barriers to trust

Broken trust in the past is probably the most common reason for the struggle many abused people have to trust again. Feelings are left very raw after abusive events, and distrust of an abuser leads to uncertainty as to the trustworthiness of anyone. This unwillingness to trust isolates a person and can create other problems, like loneliness, having no one to share with, and no way of checking out feelings and the best way forward. It can also lead to self-doubt or doubt about God.

Other barriers to trusting can include thinking that trust is impossible, too costly and should not even be attempted. This way of thinking produces despair. Despair robs one of the energy to trust due to fearing further hurt. The impact of such attitudes on a person's ability to form human relationships is profound, but the consequences in terms of the ability to relate to God may be just as great.

Learning to trust God

The God of the Bible is a loving God who sees and under-stands everything that happens on earth, and he is passionately concerned about every person he has placed in this world. The Bible informs us that he is not a distant and absent god; if God did not care about his creation, and every individual, he would not have sent his only Son, Jesus Christ, into the world. God sees and understands all the troubles and issues that face some-one who has been sexually abused. He alone knows the depth of the lonely storms faced in life, and God himself wants to rebuild hurting people from the inside out. He can repair what may, from a human perspective, seem impossible to mend.

Understandably, however, an abused person may have difficulty in trusting God. Abused people frequently put God into the same category as those humans who betrayed their position of trust by committing abuse in the first place, so proving themselves to be untrustworthy. The abused person may feel that God has let them down by not stopping the abuse from happening. However, a clear distinction must be made between an abuser and God. God, who is love, never sanctions abuse in any way. Abuse is always the result of the wilful and wrong choice of an abuser. Every individual has his own will and the capacity to choose, and that includes the capacity to make bad choices. The capacity for sin that is in each of us is a result of the fall of humanity from the perfection in which God created it, as recorded in Genesis, the first book of the Bible.[1] Were it not for the presence of sin in the world, sexual abuse would not exist. The suffering caused by abuse breaks God's heart because it was never part of his original design for any human being.

As humans we tend to believe that if God is good and he loves people, then he will make life pleasant for everyone. So when things go according to our plan and we feel happy, we conclude that God is good. However, when life is difficult and contains major traumas like abuse, we question the goodness of God and may even decide that he does not exist. However, our present-day happiness or pain is not the measure by which to assess the goodness or existence of God. The Bible affirms that God is always good and loving; the specific circumstances humans find themselves in cannot change his character. God's

---

1. Genesis 3:1-24.

love for each individual is unchanged even if the only approach to him that can be managed is full of mistrust, hurt and anger on account of the abuse that has been suffered. God is still there whilst trust is slowly growing. His patience and love go far beyond anything that the human mind can imagine.

Trusting in God does not mean that all circumstances will automatically improve or change. It is all too easy to expect that God will deliver from all ills when his promise is actually to be with those who suffer.[2] Free will in all people means that suffering may not be removed or prevented, but strength and help is available through the pain.

Learning more about God's character is helpful in enabling someone to trust him, as Heather discovered:

> I appreciate more and more of God's personal love for me. Slowly but surely I have allowed God to change my wrong perceptions about him and about myself that I was no longer content to hold on to. God began to show me new aspects of his character, and I saw his attributes through his word and in my daily experience. My trust in him grew as I found him to be completely trustworthy. I particularly struggled to believe that God loved me as an individual. From my initial repentance when I became a Christian, I have had a wonderful adventure of faith, with its ups and downs, joys and sorrows, disappointments (in me) and successes. Now I know in my head and my heart that God loves me unconditionally. The Lord challenged me once by simply saying to me, 'I will measure how much you love me by how much you trust me.'

---

2. 'When you pass through the waters, I will be with you; and when you pass through the rivers, they will not sweep over you. When you walk through the fire, you will not be burned; the flames will not set you ablaze' (Isa. 43:2).

Fatherhood

God is to be trusted because he is a good Father and a good father affirms and encourages. A father is someone who is there for his child in a protective, caring and providing role, offering security and stability. A good father is one who shows his child that the world is bigger than himself or herself. He helps the child to separate from his or her mother in a healthy way, calling the child into contact with the outside world. His love should be unconditional and never-ending, showing itself in appropriate physical, material and emotional ways. The ideal father would be one who met every expressed and unexpressed need of his child.

It's true that human fathers can fail in a variety of ways, consciously or subconsciously, mistakenly or deliberately. It is my own belief that when a child is born, God asks parents to take care of that child on his behalf, but all parents have the capacity to make mistakes and sometimes make a poor job of their God-given task. Fathers and mothers can fail, simply because they are human.

I remember one client who said she couldn't cope with the thought of having a Father in heaven as well as her own earthly dad because she was fully satisfied with her own father, who gave her everything she wanted. Much more common is the person who doesn't want to know anything about God as Father because they are unable to see that he is not like their imperfect earthly father. The abusive father who causes terrible emotional devastation, leaving damage and confusion, or the father who is present in body but isn't there for his child emotionally, causing neglect and possible rejection, can cause abused people to doubt the goodness of God as a Father. I and many of my clients have found that a living relationship with God as Father is of tremendous benefit to our health and well-being. This is because God has a plan for every person who trusts in him, and has the very best in mind for him or her.

Heather was sexually abused by her own father, and as a result had a struggle to really trust God:

Father God means everything to me now but I am utterly ashamed of how long it took me to trust him. In my particular situation, I believed I had a good daddy even though he had abused me. It never crossed my mind that his behaviour towards me was anything other than good, because of my daddy's belief in God. However, I suppressed the abuse, and long before it came to my conscious mind, I had embarked on a relationship with Jesus. I had confessed my sins and asked Jesus into my heart.

The abuse and my reactions to it had created a wall between God and me. I didn't let God too near me. When I did eventually cry out to him, he was right there and I could never have believed how loving he was and is. No, my Heavenly Father does not resemble my earthly daddy, but I tested him a few times until I was sure. He has never failed me. He has proved to me time and time again that he loves me unconditionally. He is always there for me.

At first my trust was weak, but the older I get, the more I see my need of God. I just can't face each day alone or in my own strength. I don't have what it takes. The more I receive Father God's love, the more pain is taken from me and I am set free. When the abuse I suffered rose into my conscious mind, I asked God, 'why?' Why had it happened? I wasn't angry with God, as I know some people are. I knew my daddy had a free will and he made a number of wrong choices. Father God has comforted me and lovingly healed me bit by bit. Now I am a new person, no longer a mere survivor of abuse but a victor. Father God is my strength and my stay.

God initiated a relationship with mankind from the moment of creation because of his heart of love for all human beings.

He made the first move. Father God is lavish in his love and in all his provision, and is just waiting for hurting men and women to turn to him for help.

Henry too has proved this in his experience:

Throughout my life I can see that God has gone before me and anticipated my every need. It has to be said that my Father in Heaven has always been more willing to give to me than I have been to receive. One of my favourite verses is 2 Corinthians 9:8: 'And God is able to make all grace abound to you, so that in all things at all times, having all that you need, you will abound in every good work.' My Heavenly Father's detailed care of me has been awesome. At one time in my life I was so alone and isolated – God provided me with companionship; firstly, his own presence, causing my confidence to grow to reach out to others.

At every turn I can see his loving care and evidence of his watchful eye over the minutiae of my life. Things haven't always been easy and circumstantially I've had it tough, but God has never failed me. I'm beginning to grasp more of his purposes for my life and to move forward into grasping life with both hands. Previously friends would have found me cautious and lacking self-confidence. Now my confidence and my identity is in God, my new Father, who loves me through and through. I'm even learning to love myself, which is a miracle. I can cope with my own company and am now enjoying quiet times in the presence of God. Without periods of stillness I lose my calm. God has provided me with grace, with strength, with courage, with the desire to be holy and to pray. He has provided me with a wife, which I thought I could never have, and much more. Only a loving Heavenly Father could do all this.

God's love

The experience of abuse can pollute and distort the true meaning of the word 'love'. God's love is not an impure or lustful love; rather God's love is pure, because God is perfect and without sin; it's not possible for God to hate or to harm. God always has our best interests at heart, not necessarily what we want, but what he, in his divine wisdom, knows we need in order to be transformed into his image. The true nature of God's love is not a matter of speculation; it can be seen lived out in the life of Jesus Christ. God moved toward us in love when his Son, Jesus, demonstrated what real love is by dying on the cross, taking the punishment for all our sins. Jesus also rose from the dead and is still alive in heaven, which is proof that he is more than a mere man. 'After the Lord Jesus had spoken to them, he was taken up into heaven and he sat at the right hand of God' (Mark 16:19).[3] That kind of love is more concerned for the loved one than for itself, in other words, utterly unselfish. Romans 8:32 tells us that God loved us enough to give us his own Son – 'will he not also, along with him, graciously give us all things?' This love and generosity is extended to anyone who turns to him in trusting faith. This is of special significance to those who have been sexually abused, as no life circumstance, event or trauma changes the fact of God's marvellous love.

Henry found the experience of God's love life-transforming:

> My tendency to see things negatively was with me from a young age. At my lowest point I felt very depressed and even contemplated suicide. I realise now that it was the love of God that saved me from taking such drastic action. I also realise now that it was God's love that wooed me and brought me through into full healing. At first I did not see this in my life, but as I learned to take my eyes off myself and focus them

---

3. See also Acts 1:9-11; Hebrews 4:14-16.

on him, then I experienced his great and very personal love for me. This love gave me a desire to pursue him and all the healing that he had to offer. No human love could ever have compared with it.

Romans 8:35-39 clearly tells that there is nothing - not even the most horrific experiences - that can separate us from the love of God in Christ Jesus. Anyone can be 'more than a conqueror' (Rom. 8:37), even someone suffering from abuse.

God's presence

It has been amazing, when working with clients who have been sexually abused and have chosen to follow Jesus, to see the help they gain from either remembering or realising for the first time that God is present with them at all times. A relationship with God on a day-to-day basis can be fostered regardless of circumstances and emotions. A person may not feel the presence of God, but that does not alter the truth that God the Holy Spirit indwells Christians and so is with them at all times and listens to them. Furthermore, it is God the Holy Spirit who, when invited, inspires thought, reasoning, imagination and hope. It is he who provides strength and grace to believe for the impossible. This truth is based on what God has promised in his Word, the Bible, and it is that which the Christian needs to hold on to when feelings and knowledge are in conflict.

Listening is such an important aspect of living, but it is often much neglected. It can be the case that abused people have not been listened to, or have not been heard when trying to convey what was happening to them. It is life-giving to know in one's own experience that God always listens, even when humans have failed. If that is not enough, God lets us know in his Word (the Bible) how accessible he is: 'Here I am! I stand at the door and knock. If anyone hears my voice and opens the door, I will come in and eat with him, and he with me' (Rev. 3:20). Jesus has promised to be with anyone who sincerely depends on him for help.[4] This divine companion can bring much comfort and reassurance to people as they embark on the process of healing. The Psalmist tells us that God is very near (Ps. 119:151); as someone once said, God is only a prayer away.

Prayer

Prayer, which is a two-way conversation between a person and God, is something that has had increasing importance in my own life with the passage of time. Many of my clients have also found prayer to be helpful. However, it must be acknowledged that some people cannot pray because of abuse. They are numb, and accessing God feels impossible. Sometimes it might be the task of the counsellor to do the praying on behalf of the client, with their full permission, until such time they are able to pray themselves. It is a tremendous comfort to leave burdens with God in prayer, especially when answers are hard to find. Through Jesus we have immediate access to God, who hears us and listens whenever we pray. Prayer is a phenomenal and unique resource.

One client, whom I will refer to as James, discovered prayer for himself. When he was at the very end of his tether, after being abused by both grandparents, James cried out to God and asked him to make himself real to him. James was not inclined to trust anyone, but knew he could not go on with such pain inside his heart. James began to talk to God out of desperation and discovered he was indeed real, and that he was there for him. James made it a habit to pour out his heart to God and he wrote down some of his prayers. The sense he had that God was real gave him hope and sufficient confidence to

---

4. 'And surely I am with you always, to the very end of the age' (Matt. 28:20).

ask for help at school. Then things really began to change for the better. James was taken from the care of his grandparents and began to sleep far better, doing well at school, and he found peace within himself. His reliance on God grew, and he sought out other Christians to help and encourage him.

God listens to us at any time. During Christ's time on earth, he attracted multitudes not merely by what he said, but equally by his willingness to listen to individuals' distressing circumstances. After hearing the full story, he would respond with an appropriate word or touch. Jesus comforted Lazarus's sisters after Lazarus died (John 11:19). In the case of a woman he met beside a well, Jesus heard not only her words but understood completely her unsatisfactory and unsatisfying lifestyle and offered her living water which would always satisfy her thirst – eternal life.[5] Jesus can do exactly the same for those distressed by the effects of abuse.

First steps towards God

To build a relationship with God, there has to be an understanding that every human being is a sinner. Perhaps that sounds outrageous! Most of us imagine that what someone has done to us is far worse than anything we would ever do, but this is a myth. The fact is that everyone is capable of committing grievous sins. The Bible says: 'If we claim to be without sin, we deceive ourselves and the truth is not in us' (1 John 1:8). Romans 3:23 confirms that 'There is no difference, for all have sinned and fall short of the glory of God'. In God's eyes, all sin is serious, because in essence sin is the failure to obey God and live in relationship with him. Which of us can claim to always obey even the first commandment, which is to love God with all our hearts and minds?

---

5. 'If anyone is thirsty, let him come to me and drink' (John 7:37).

People who have been abused have certainly been sinned against, but that does not mean there is nothing in their lives for them to confess to God; they may need to repent of their own wrong choices, or sinful responses to others' wrongdoing. It is also important to understand that a distinction has to be made between what the abused person is responsible for in relation to his or her reactions to the abuser, and what the abuser has to sort out with God. Sometimes an abused person will try to take all the blame for what happened, but there is no benefit in repenting for the abuser's sin, and in reality it cannot be done, because we are all responsible for our own sin before God.

Yet how can anyone be forgiven? If people continue through life sinning and not dealing with it, there will be consequences, just as there were for Adam and Eve. The Bible tells us that everlasting life is God's free gift to mankind, 'For the wages of sin is death, but the gift of God is eternal life in Christ Jesus our Lord' (Rom. 6:23). Jesus came to this earth as a human being, yet he was still fully divine, which means that he has the authority to offer every individual the free gift of forgiveness and salvation. However, there is no benefit in being given a gift unless it is received and used. When Jesus, the sinless man, died on the cross, he took the punishment each one of us deserves from a just and righteous God for all our sins, and he shared in all our torn emotions, all our sorrows. We know that God accepted his sacrifice in our place because God raised Jesus from the dead, which is well documented in the Bible and was never disproved by the Roman or Jewish authorities of the day. The Christian faith hinges on this truth.

To be connected to God, we need firstly to find a solution to sin, which creates barriers between people and God. Repenting does this, as we come to God admitting that we fall very far short of his standards in the way we think and speak and act. The Bible assures us that 'if we confess our sins, he is faithful and just and will forgive us our sins and purify us from all unrighteousness' (1 John 1:9).

God delights in a repentant heart, and he gently prompts us towards repenting so that there can be a relationship with him. As repentance is not a feeling or an attitude of heart that can be self-generated, we need to depend on God to give us a repentant heart. The greatest gift of God to people is that of forgiveness of sin and access to him as a result of the barrier of sin being dealt with. There is then a need to receive God's forgiveness by accepting it as real. The next step, and often a difficult one, is choosing to forgive one's self. It seems that being forgiven by God, which is miraculous, is something that can be accepted, but we have more trouble choosing to let ourselves off the hook when we are consciously aware of sin or wrongdoing. It seems preferable to constantly go over the old ground of remembering how awful it was to err. Learning to receive forgiveness from God and to stop reminding ourselves of our sin are two separate and essential miracles that pave the way for a healing, growing relationship with God.

When Heather came to God in repentance, she found that she needed to radically alter what she believed about the character of God:

> My picture of God was well and truly tarnished. I knew in my head that God was a God of love, but from my experience of abuse and from my religious upbringing, I saw him as hard, cold and remote. It took me some considerable time to work out that I had developed wrong beliefs about God because of the pain in my heart. I then had to repent of my unhelpful reactions to those who sinned against me, and to those who helped me form a wrong understanding of the character of God.
>
> My life was revolutionised when I came to God and confessed my sin. I asked Jesus to forgive me and to come

into my heart. Beyond the shadow of a doubt, he came. My circumstances did not improve; nothing had changed except my heart. When I caught a glimpse of what it cost Jesus to die on my behalf, I saw my sin from his perspective. I could not go on without dealing with it. I felt deep pain that my sin should cost so much to sort out. God took me at my word and he came into my life. That first step was in my teenage years. Increasingly, as I have walked with God, he has revealed to me other ways that I have hurt him.

God longs to welcome us home just like the prodigal son.[6] Being 'at home' with God is choosing to take that one step towards him. To make that move towards God is one of the most important choices anyone can make, and when we make it, the Lord comes to us in a special way that furthers our relationship with him. A wonderful verse that demonstrates God's desire to make his home with us is John 14:23: 'Jesus replied, "If anyone loves me, he will obey my teaching. My Father will love him, and we will come to him and make our home with him".'

This chapter has tried to look at the subject of trusting God, not an easy one for the abused person, but worth pursuing because it lays a foundation for building a new life. Flora has often had doubts about God and his love for her, but she has never given up trying to making sense of it all:

I was taught as a child that Christians must trust God, and so I did. I trusted him to keep me safe, and he didn't do so. I couldn't risk admitting this, so I split the abuse off from my faith and kept it buried out of sight where it couldn't make me a 'bad Christian'. I'm still trying to integrate the furious, abandoned child, who believes God let her down, and the reluctant older woman who finds, after much heart-searching, that somehow she is still following Christ. What do I now mean by trust?

6. The story of the prodigal son is found in Luke 15.

118

I mean trusting that in God, somehow, incomprehensibly, is a place where it all makes sense. I can believe that without having to rewrite my history, and when I do believe (which is by no means always), I have an anchor to a Rock in the midst of all the storms and anguish. That's worth having.

CHAPTER 6

REBUILDING TRUST HORIZONTALLY

Rebuilding trust with people

The damage done to the ability to form relationships is one of the most distressing and debilitating consequences of sexual abuse. Since trust has been broken in the past, it can seem impossible to ever trust anyone again, especially when, as is often the case, the abuser was someone who should have been totally trustworthy, perhaps an uncle, aunt, family friend, or even, tragically, a parent. The betrayal of such trust causes untold heartache. However, the experience of many I have counselled is that, hard though it may be, trusting again is manageable if it is based on knowing about the character of the one in whom trust is to be placed. It can take considerable time to learn to trust again; it does not happen automatically or in an instant. In exceptional circumstances it can take a number of years.

One of the recurrent themes of abused people is, 'I won't ever trust again.' Often they have made what amounts to an inner vow never to trust anyone again. However, acknowledging the existence of an inner vow and dealing with it can be a crucial step in moving towards healing. If such a vow is not given up, it can have an ongoing effect on decisions and can become a controlling and even crippling factor in a person's life.

Daisy's failure to trust could be seen in all her relationships. Friends and family found her to be unpredictable and inconsistent. No one knew where he or she stood with her. This was in fact a character change that took place immediately after she was raped, which was something Daisy was not prepared to explain to her friends. She felt especially angry that her rapist had caused her problems in the area of trusting people. It took considerable effort to choose to consider trusting anybody. What she eventually managed to do in order to start renewing trust was to take very small, manageable steps over a period of time, and to build each improvement on top of the last one. For example, Daisy learned to talk a little with her best friend and share a bit more of herself. When this selective sharing felt safe to her and the confidences were not broken, she then felt she could move on by choosing to share a bit more. This process did not happen overnight and it took about ten months before she could actually voice the fact that she had been raped to her friend. The reward of building this relationship of trust was a feeling of immense relief once the truth was told. At the same time Daisy tried to speak more to her mother, but when that did not work out, she realised that this was more a consequence of her mother's problems than her own. Whereas previously her mother's struggle would have felt as if it was really hers, now she understood that one day her mother might be able to talk more deeply, but was in fact at this stage choosing not to do so.

Every person is unique, and each abused person has different mountains to climb and conquer. The small steps needed as rebuilding progresses will vary, depending on the individual. One man I counselled could not cope with his church Bible studies because there were women present. After Roy confided in his pastor, an arrangement was made to have a small male group for him to study with. The next step, in consultation with the pastor, was to attend a mixed meeting in the church hall. When he was ready, he tried to go to a house meeting, which was one where he thought he might feel relatively 'safe'. At first this didn't work out and Roy left the room after about twenty minutes. Each week, if he could face it, he would try to go to the meeting. Roy considered it a great victory when he stayed in the room for an entire hour. After about six months of this, Roy was able to sit through the entire meeting, feeling comfortable and relaxed. During counselling Roy was able to derive support from his counsellor and his pastor, as well as sympathetic group members.

What are relationships?

Relationships fulfil a variety of functions. It is through relationships that human beings give and receive love; it is where we learn to laugh and cry and share together. Relationships are the way humans interact, help one another and develop as individuals. As the Bible puts it, 'Two are better than one, because they have a good return for their work: If one falls down, his friend can help him up. But pity the man who falls and has no one to help him up!' (Eccles. 4:9-10).

Human beings conduct a wide variety of relationships, from the superficial to the meaningful and intimate. The craving for intimacy in relationships is part of the fabric of every human being, and most people are born with the desire to relate and to make friends, unless the pain has been so great in life that an inner vow has been made not to let anyone get close again.

Pain can be expected occasionally in all relationships, even in good ones. Interacting with other people can be tough going at times, because relating is a challenge and brings with it the possibility of disappointment and frustration. When we are close to someone, and care for him or her very much, the potential to hurt, or to be hurt, is heightened. When a relationship is embarked upon, involvement and communication increase. As more is shared, the relationship develops and more risks are taken. It goes without saying that in many relationships the joy and pleasure increases as time goes on. In the situation of a relationship breakdown, or when something goes wrong, the risks are greater the deeper the relationship has been, because there is more shared knowledge of one another and it is possible that one or the other could use that information in a damaging way.

This can be particularly worrying for someone who has suffered abuse. Regardless of who abused them, the abused person's relationships with other people almost inevitably suffer. The grievous destruction that takes place within a life because of sexual abuse can make achieving and maintaining good relationships seem almost too formidable. There can be difficulty in trusting, in sharing from the heart and in taking other people at face value. The losses and robbery within relationships because of abuse have been such that relating to others, something that should be so natural, becomes complex and fraught.

For this reason it is wise to proceed slowly when developing new friendships, allowing time for trust to be established, and consciously working to keep relationships healthy through open and honest communication. This would mean saying if there was something that was disturbing or uncomfortable about the relationship. Keeping short accounts is the way to build a healthy relationship where both people are able to be true to their own feelings.

Boundaries in relationships
Whilst relationships are a vital part of human existence, everyone needs to know the social rules within which they operate, and these may vary from culture to culture. Boundaries are an

important part of these generally understood rules. These are limits we place on others and ourselves which help us to maintain a sense of individuality, separateness and independence. When we are children, we learn to separate ourselves from other people and to experience ourselves as a single, independent human being. A part of learning boundaries is determining what is ours and what is not ours. One of the things that children own is their body; they learn to believe that it is their own, and that no one else is allowed to touch, use or disturb it without permission. These rules, or boundaries, are often carried into adulthood. However, very often children who have been abused are not allowed, or haven't had the chance, to learn these boundaries. Sexual or physical abuse leads to confusion over these very basic rules of ownership. Children who have been abused may have been taught that their body can be hurt and abused or manipulated by others. They learn that their bodies are not their own, and as a result their boundaries are variable or non-existent.

In order to start relating to other people, someone who has experienced the violation of sexual abuse needs to be able to feel safe in himself or herself. In order to do this, personal boundaries need to be in place. Every individual has a separate and distinct personality, with a will, with responsibilities, and with particular character gifts and traits. In life we each need to be ourselves and at the same time be connected to other people in ways that will preserve and enhance each person's own identity and individuality. The person who is healthy in body, soul and spirit will have healthy boundaries in each of these areas of life. Everyone needs to allow access to the right people, the ones with whom they are comfortable, by having appropriate boundaries. Physically, everyone needs to be happy about who they allow to touch them and to know where their personal comfort zone is. This may include, for instance, how close they feel comfortable standing next to someone else. Emotional boundaries are about having appropriate protection for the heart, especially when it has been previously wounded. An abused person has to choose whom to allow into their hearts. Spiritually, everyone needs to be aware of what influences they open themselves up to and to whom they are accountable. Sexually abused people sometimes want to tell everybody their story with all the details. This makes them too vulnerable. It is extremely helpful for the person to learn who to tell and who not to tell. Many abused people have later regretted sharing their story too freely, as it can never be untold.

Poor boundaries
It is very common for abused people to struggle with the whole issue of boundaries. This is not surprising, given the damaging effects of sexual abuse on self-esteem, self-image and self-acceptance. Poor or inappropriate boundaries can create stress, deplete energy, encourage false guilt and exacerbate low self-esteem. Decision-making faculties may have been bypassed or damaged, and as a result the abused person does not know how to set limits, how to say 'no', or sometimes even to know how he or she feels. Injury through abuse to the physical body, injury to attitudes, choices, thoughts and feelings, can inhibit the ability to set appropriate boundaries. Good boundaries are needed to make relationships work, and many of these difficulties can be greatly helped by building new personal boundaries.

I remember Anne, a lady whose almost total lack of boundaries led to a chaotic lifestyle. She wanted to have more control in her life, to shed unnecessary burdens, to learn to make right choices and to have self-confidence. Counselling was revolutionary for her, because her need of boundaries became clear. For instance, she would ask intrusive questions of work colleagues and would expect someone to accompany her to the toilet, because at home she was never alone. She was unaware that this was totally unacceptable behaviour in the workplace, and had to learn what was and was not acceptable.

Having left her abusive home situation, Anne experienced difficulty in living independently, because she had no idea how to relate to flatmates and was unable to protect herself from friends who took advantage of her. Like many abused people, Anne needed to learn that other people's boundaries have to be respected if relationships are to be healthy. Sometimes people have to modify their own boundaries out of consideration for others. For instance, someone whose boundaries include a ban on being kissed by anyone in greeting may have to realise that there is nothing threatening or offensive in being kissed on both cheeks by those who are used to that in their own culture.

Living with a poor set of boundaries can lead to a variety of problems over time. An unhealthy dependency or co-dependency sometimes develops between people. Many sexually abused people are familiar with being over-involved emotionally with close friends, which can lead to them expecting their friend to tell them who they are and give them meaning. Co-dependency is a little more complex and can be described as a deep need to please another person, and involves a desperate need to be needed.[1] It can also involve an abused person controlling a friend, or vice versa. Emotional dependency and co-dependency are, therefore, relational and emotional traps in relating which are consequences of poor boundaries.

Another common problem is that the need for a meaningful relationship can be so urgent that it results in appropriate boundaries being ignored. When I met Vera, who was a most

1. Further reading.: Pat Springle, *Co-dependency*, Rapha Publishing/ Word Inc. 1995, Houston and Dallas; Hemfelt, Minirth, and Meier, *Love is a Choice*, Nashville, Thomas Nelson Inc 1989; Lori Rentzel, *Emotional Dependency*, IVP.

attractive young girl, she had a desperate need for a meaningful relationship as a result of having been abused by her step-father from the age of ten. In order to escape this situation, she married the first available man, who happened to be her step-brother. Her lack of understanding about boundaries meant she failed to see him simply as a brother and allowed him to overstep appropriate boundaries. Later, Vera felt she had married the wrong man by ignoring what she really knew to be true in her heart – that she did not love him and in fact did not like him.[2]

Healthy boundaries

To begin to create healthy boundaries it is vital to learn to say 'no'. No matter what age someone is, it is never too late to learn to say this to an abuser, or within any abusive or compromising situation. It can be incredibly hard to learn to say 'no' when the abuser has not heard this 'no' in the past, but it is a myth to believe that having boundaries or saying 'no' is selfish. Rather it is to do with one's self-respect, dignity and development. There is no need to always do what other people expect or require. There is a need to love ourselves enough to establish bounda-ries, which will grant us the freedom to think and feel our *own* thoughts and emotions. It will take time, patience and perse-verance to begin to learn new boundaries, and this is a process that can be greatly helped by the support of other people.

Heather has some experience of trying to set new boundaries and learning to say 'no'. Perhaps her story will be an encouragement:

I didn't realise that I could say 'no'. It felt like I only existed in relation to others' involvement with me. They were the

2. For further reading see Dr Henry Cloud & Dr John Townsend, *Boundaries*, Zondervan, Michigan, 1992.

significant ones; I was inferior. I thought I was being humble, but now I see that rather I hated myself. Counselling helped me to see this and supported me as I dealt with these issues. Layer by layer I began to see that I didn't have the choice when I was younger, but now I could begin to set in place appropriate boundaries. I needed necessary space for myself. It used to be that I couldn't stand my own company – I would always be around other people, letting them choose what we would do. I felt crippled. Saying 'no' to a social event was impossible, and yet the last thing I wanted to do was go. My image of myself was that I was fluid, pulled in this and that direction, with no firm thoughts or feelings or opinions. How wrong I was. I do have the ability to choose, to say 'no', to be my own person.

It's important to me now to be far clearer in my head that I am valued by God and that he loves me. How much longer it has taken me to know this in my heart as well as my head! I will say 'no' if I feel uncomfortable now, but goodness, what a time it took me to realise that it was okay to say 'no'. Boundaries have become a vital part of my life. I have become strong in knowing who I am as a person of worth and dignity, knowing who I am in Christ and in knowing who I am as a person in my own right. I am also no longer fluid, no longer so dominated. I broke the power of my abuser when I learned to have my own opinions, my own space. That's another new thing for me. I can cope now with my own company, my own thoughts. In fact I've settled knowing that I need this space each day, for my own sake. I have a wee place in the house that's mine alone, and I am comfortable to be there, to talk to God there and to face up to the vulnerability of being on my own. I don't know how I lived without this space before. I've created it by saying that it is important to have boundaries.

There are particular skills required for the appropriate setting of boundaries so that the abused person can be comfortable and in control (in the right sense) of relationships. Time has to be taken to gain awareness of setting up and establishing new personal boundaries. It is best to tackle them one at a time rather than many at once. Each boundary can be a stepping-stone for the next one. It is helpful for abused people to establish who they are and who they are not, rather than who they are as defined by their abuser. One of the best ways forward in this area is to learn to say 'no', and to learn to overcome the fear of saying 'no'. This fear is connected to having been controlled by the abuser or by the effects of the abuse. Saying 'no' can take a lot of practice and perseverance. Clients have often reported saying 'yes', when everything in them was shouting 'no', but over time, and with encouragement and support, saying 'no' gradually becomes easier.

A lady I worked with, who I will call Judy, was so upset at her sexually abusive husband that she decided to make herself unattractive in order to stop the abuse. The abuse didn't stop, but her internal decision went very deep within her. Judy became very depressed and was unable to do anything in her life to look or feel good. One of the first things we tried was to get her to wash her hair. It was greasy and hadn't been washed for a very long time. It took four weeks of little adjustments in her thinking to allow her to fill a basin with water. It took a further two weeks for Judy to actually wash her hair. We talked through how it felt for her. Judy realised after she washed her hair that she did not believe she was entitled to even feel good about herself. When she learned to wash her hair and look in the mirror afterwards, Judy could see that she was making progress. We followed the same principles in all the areas she struggled in, and in each and through time there was betterment. Negative thoughts became positive, and ultimately the depression lifted. Judy learned to create boundaries with her husband even though she began to look after herself and looked good again. Her attractiveness was no longer something that meant her husband would abuse her, because that was not the reason for the abuse in the first place. Judy got well and her husband learned that there were new barriers which prevented his abusive behaviour. He learned that when Judy said 'no', she meant 'no', and that he would have to think again. In telling a story like this there is the danger of making it all sound as though the end result was easily gained. Not so. In this situation Judy earned every inch through sheer grit and determination. Her bravery in challenging old negative thoughts and unhealthy boundaries was extraordinary. In learning to be true to herself and having healthy boundaries, Judy decided it was essential to have some space between her and her husband. This marriage has not been mended because of her husband's unwillingness to change his behaviour. However, Judy is a much happier person, the source of abuse has been removed and little by little she is becoming more whole as a person. Looking back, she can hardly believe that her healing began when she learned to wash her hair!

Changes are more than possible when it is realised that every unhelpful and negative thought can be turned around. The abused person has to challenge every negative thought when it comes and then consistently replace it with a positive attitude. A process like this can take many months, or even years, and can be very hard work, because changing negative ways of thinking is an uphill climb, especially when the negatives have been around for a long time. It is helpful to learn what moral values are to be adhered to, so that limits become more obvious and priorities can be set, establishing which limit and boundary should be worked on first. There is great advantage in being pro-active in this area, having plans and strategies thought through before a situation arises.

Learning to be true to self and honest with others are vital steps in moving forward. Harold, a young man who was abused by his mother over a long period of time, managed to live independently. He still wanted to have contact with his mother but was concerned that her past behaviour would be repeated. He would arrange a visit with her in advance to make sure someone else was around, or meet in a public place. This was a boundary he insisted on because of his values. He wanted to have a moral relationship with his mother, but her standards were different to his. It was a constant trial to keep his boundaries with her. Harold insisted that he was going to value himself and kept this boundary in place.

I can just imagine an abused person reading this section on boundaries and saying to himself or herself, 'How can I possibly change in this area? It's such a big part of my life. I'll need to change what I think, learn how I feel, to know what I want and live very differently.' When someone embarks on a new stage of healing, they can feel that they will never get to the end of the road. However, like Judy, Harold and many others I have known, it is possible to get there, and anyone who sets out on this road will be all the richer and wiser for learning to establish boundaries, which promote health and well-being. Healthy boundaries will also allow for the development of healthy relationships.

Choices

Adopting boundaries involves making choices, and this is something abused people can struggle with because of the painful things done against their will in the past. As humans, we are created with the power to make our own decisions and to act on them. It is incredibly hard to face making choices when there has been abuse, because it robs the person of the right to choose. This is destructive and can almost disable a person from making choices at all.

The way forward is to make right choices based on what is known to be true. For instance, one of my clients went to the police to report on what was happening at home. When her abuser threatened her, she reneged on her complaint, because she feared for her life. The clear truth was that she was under the influence of her abuser and that if she did not make the right choice to get out of this situation the abuse would continue. However, after this first attempt she sought my support and was able to follow through on her complaint to the police. The right choice was followed through and she was able to live independently without ongoing abuse. All the time she was scared and tense, but knew she should do what was right. Like many abused people, Sadie discovered that in following through with right decisions feelings do catch up in time.

Vince is someone who had always found it hard to make choices that would promote health and well-being in his life. He was brought up on abuse; it was all he ever knew. He found it hard to trust authority figures because of painful experiences in his early years and when the challenge came to choose to trust a new employer, Vince failed at the starting post. He was out of the job within a week when he reacted with uncontrolled anger towards his employer. Then Vince decided he really needed to change his life for the better. With reluctance and trepidation Vince went to see a counsellor to talk through his problems. Never before had he experienced someone being willing to listen to his whole life story. Just being listened to helped him feel of value and worth. Trust grew in this relationship and Vince began to understand some of the root issues in his life, including the anger he struggled to manage. His parents and teachers had ridiculed him over the years and Vince was tired of being hurt. When the time came for him to start another job he had more of an idea about how to relate. He chose to move house and start afresh in order to take up his new post. All these choices, which others might have made automatically, were milestones in his healing and would have been impossible for him in the past. Vince had learned about healthy boundaries and tried to put all this into practice. The big test came in the first month when a colleague deliberately sabotaged his task for the day, which meant that Vince would not earn his weekly bonus. He was very angry, but chose to deal with it in a controlled manner instead of flying off the handle. Vince is determined to build on what he had learned and has now been in work for a year. He has a couple of new mates and is slowly rebuilding his life.

Progress will be very slow in this area if the abused person waits until his or her emotions are in line with the choice he wants to make. Often the right choice has to be made with gritted teeth, and it may be that the emotions will agree with the choice made only after some days, weeks, months or even longer. Christians often find it helps to pray for their will to be strengthened, especially when the right choice is clear but the will to follow it through is somewhat lacking. This prayer can be repeated daily until progress is seen.

The choice of forgiveness

Probably the hardest choice of all is choosing to forgive, but unforgiveness can slow down recovery from abuse and can sometimes be a causal factor in depression and many other symptoms that come from abuse.[3] Forgiving involves giving up any thought of revenge and to choose not to hold the abuse against the abuser. Forgiveness is a very important stage to come to and needs to be approached with much care. The whole concept of forgiving is both complex and thorny for anyone who has been sexually abused. However, consideration needs to be given to forgiving the abuser.

Early on in counselling we usually try to set out the possible ground that needs to be covered for the person to move towards wholeness. We always say that forgiving the abuser is

---

3. See *Unforgiveness* in chapter 3.

expedient for the abused person's healing, but is not something that should be embarked on lightly or without a great deal of thought. Expecting someone to forgive can be raised far too early in the counselling process. It is all too easy to suggest forgiving to someone who hasn't quite come to the place of knowing who it is he or she is forgiving and for what. Forgiveness can only be part of the healing process after there is an understanding of what was involved in the abuse, the nature of the wrongs and where the responsibility lies. Otherwise it will be counterproductive. If the abused person has not yet blamed the abuser and recognised feelings of betrayal and anger, seeming forgiveness can actually be a form of denial. It is as though the person says, 'If I just forgive then all this will go away and I won't have to face the pain.' Sadly, such thinking is not productive, and the pain simply goes underground to be accessed at another time.

Forgiveness is rarely a one-off event, and is about overcoming the past, a way of moving on. Often the choice to forgive has to be made over and over, as different aspects of the abuse surface. It is a process that can take a long time; weeks, months or even years.

Many of my clients, such as Priscilla, have experienced this process:

> I learned that the closure I sought came from forgiving my abuser. I discovered that closure was up to me as I faced emotional giants. It was a long and painful road, but I was determined not to paper over cracks. Resolution was what I wanted. In my own heart I had the capacity to move on by choosing to forgive my abuser. He no longer has the same hold over me.

Difficult though it is to learn to forgive, many, like Henry, testify that it is well worth the effort:

No matter how sincerely I have forgiven, that decision has had to be reaffirmed each time more pain has come up to the surface. I have not found forgiving to be a magical key to serenity and relief because of the anguish forgiving has caused, but it has drawn a definite line under the past and ultimately has made me a stronger person. I guess that I forgave primarily for my own sake. The result has been that I no longer carry the burdens of resentment, bitterness and unresolved anger or grief – all of which were crippling me.

Heather also came to understand that she needed to consider forgiving her father:

For many years I did not realise that I had to think about forgiving my daddy for his wrongdoing. Once I clearly saw that the abuse was his responsibility, I forgave him in a general way. After a few more years, I saw there was a need to be more specific. I got out a large notebook and over a good number of days wrote down everything I could remember in detail. I also drew pictures to describe some of my losses. I was recommended to choose to forgive even although I did not feel like forgiving. This I did in prayer. Then I wrote across each page 'forgiven' and dated it. The pages were of no further use to me, so I destroyed them. The sting of the wrongs was lessened that day. I have had a lot of other things to deal with since, but forgiving my daddy was a real step in the right direction. It uncluttered my life.

Forgiveness allows the hurt to be in the past and doesn't allow it into the future. It also means emotional freedom from the abuser, the destructive relationship, and the hurt and pain that came with it. In order to forgive it has to be understood that the past cannot be changed. Rather, the abused person has to grieve for what can never be. The abuse cannot be undone, but forgiveness can release the hurting person to begin to take back responsibility for the choices that are to be made from here on. The goal is no longer to live life round the abuse, but rather to move on into other experiences of life. The ultimate in forgiveness is to pray that God blesses the abuser. That may seem humanly impossible, but with God all things are possible.

One of the best examples I have encountered of making a right choice in the area of forgiveness, despite contradictory feelings, was a lady whom I shall call Lily. She was so angry with her abuser that she had no intention ever of forgiving him. Then circumstances allowed her to meet a man who had abused someone else. This had a life–changing effect on them both. Lily told him exactly how she felt about her abuser and all the damage he had left her to cope with. Apparently this former abuser used Lily's emotions to help him take more responsibility for what he had done to the person he had abused. After this meeting Lily seemed to feel that some of her anger had left her, and she began to think that one day she might consider forgiving her abuser. She took a further step by committing herself to forgive sometime, when the time felt right. Each one of these shifts in her thinking was a huge step for her. In prayer, with God's help, Lily eventually chose to forgive her abuser, even though she still had very strong feelings about all that had happened. Feelings are not eradicated just because a person has made a conscious decision to forgive.

For Lily, it was as if a light had been switched on. Slowly, almost imperceptibly, Lily felt a burden had been lifted from her. After many weeks she felt her entire being was in agreement with her decision to forgive her abuser. In many ways Lily has not looked back and is now contemplating choices that she would never have imagined possible. Her life is on a new footing, as she has worked hard to make right and healthy choices, based on what she knows to be true, regardless of how she feels.

Difficulties with forgiveness

Some people have a problem with forgiveness because they see it as implying that the abusive behaviour was acceptable or that it didn't really hurt. Abuse, as we have seen, is always wrong, always hurtful, and forgiveness does not mean condoning the abuser's actions. An abuser will never be worthy of forgiveness – neither is any other human worthy for 'all have sinned' (Rom. 3:23).

The fact that someone chooses to forgive does not mean further abuse will be excused in the future. Neither does it mean that the abused person gives up the right to initiate or participate in legal proceedings, because it is important that others are protected from abusers.

Another issue that causes people to be reluctant to forgive is the misconception that forgiveness and reconciliation go together. Reconciliation is about the restoration of relationship, but is not an automatic consequence of forgiving. In fact, it should not be considered if there is an absence of long-term change in attitude and behaviour on the part of the abuser. Being unwilling to reconcile does not necessarily indicate a reluctance to forgive. The abuser would have to have a change of direction and take responsibility for the abuse, taking the blame and understanding something of the effects that abuse has had. Forgiveness and opening up to further hurt are quite different issues. Trusting again, and having a renewed relationship with the abuser should be embarked on only after much thought and consideration. I have seen successful reconciliation in some circumstances, but in other situations it has created havoc.[4]

---

4. For further reading on reconciliation see Dr Henry Cloud & Dr John Townsend, *Boundaries*, Zondervan, Michigan, 1992.

Family abuse

As we have seen, learning to relate well to other people has a very important role to play in recovery from sexual abuse, and nowhere are relationships more important than in a family. When abuse occurs with a relative or someone well known, the issue of forgiveness becomes even more complex. Ongoing contact may be required at family events and this can be very difficult emotionally, because it is a constant reminder of what happened and emphasises the great betrayal of trust that has occurred. It is this element of betrayal which makes the thought of forgiving such a challenge, but doing so is all the more vital to recovery. However, even when someone has chosen to forgive, it cannot be expected that such pain will go away overnight.

When abuse takes place within a family there can be all sorts of issues to unravel that are different from those when abuse is by a stranger. There is the fact that the abuser was someone who ought to have been trustworthy, and this causes real heartache. There can be a tendency for those abused in this way to turn to deviant behaviour, as no other way can be found to express how they feel. Family abuse affects everyone – children, parents, spouses, grandparents and the wider family circle. A brother or sister may feel undue guilt for not having been abused. There can be a great deal of agony for family members as well as the abused person. Often I have counselled the relatives of abused people who have had many issues to work through in their own right. The abuse may have been secret, but that in itself causes strains and tensions in relationships. The bearing of that kind of secret can be intolerable. Too often the abused person does not seek help or know where to turn.

In the restoration of people who have been abused within their families, there is no set formula about the rightness or wrongness of exposing the truth about the abuse to other family members. Some situations demand silence, whilst others require speaking out, honesty and openness, to enable others who may also have been hurt to have an opportunity of moving towards healing. In Heather's situation, for good reasons that confidentiality does not allow me to write about, the most loving thing has been not to disclose the fact of her abuse to the rest of her family. Heather has dealt a deathblow to denial in herself, but has left God to deal with her family as and when he chooses. To disclose or not to disclose is a question that needs to be approached prayerfully and cautiously, both having equal merit in different situations.

I recall Maud, who came for counselling and decided to tell her family that she had been raped. The emotional energy expended in keeping the rape a secret was not helping Maud to get well. Maud did not live with her parents, and following her disclosure they seemed to be too shocked and full of their own issues to be of much help. However, Maud was amazed at how her grandmother supported her through the bad and good days in the years that followed. The friend she shared a flat with was also told about Maud's experience and did everything she could to support her. In thinking back, Maud is glad that she did speak about what had happened to her, because her friend and grandmother then supported her. She had two people she could share with and this made her parents' reaction less hurtful.

My best teachers over the years have been my clients, who through their own agonies have taught me that it is not possible to judge other situations. Family dynamics are always complex, and what would be right for one could be wrong for another. This is why good counsel, support and wisdom are often needed. Of course, if a child is being abused or thought to be at risk of sexual abuse in their family, action must be taken to report this to the authorities. There is a moral obligation to do so.

Heather, in writing about her upbringing, describes how the brokenness she experienced stemmed from things that were wrong in her own family:

> I was longing for love and thought it was romantic love I needed, but my craving was actually for real family love. Not incestuous love, but genuine care and compassion. Looking back, the absence of real family love was my greatest lack. The absence of it had hit me, the absence of decent love and doing ordinary things. The absence of love and right relationships was another deficit in my life. I saw a picture of this not long ago, when I observed a right relationship between a brother and a sister – appropriately distant, appropriately loving. Through this I had a big healing crisis. I felt God's presence, I was able to tell my friend; she was there for me too (God has his representatives among human beings!). My friend listened, held me and didn't go away. I felt secure and safe enough in our relationship to be free to cry, to grieve for the absence of the normal, the ordinary, and to cry out what was previously silent pain and tears. Healing came through the love of Jesus.
>
> Today I'm facing up to the pain. I will no longer eat the brokenness of unreality and denial. I'm so familiar with it, but it chokes me now. I much prefer the reality and truth that are now being revealed. I'm rightly naming the pain, I'm calling it what it is – it's the absence of the ordinary. In facing the pain, Jesus has lifted the sting of it from me and I am freed. The pain hasn't just miraculously disappeared, but I am aware that God is helping me to make sense of my brokenness and that of my family, and I am learning to live on the other side of it.

Family life

Whilst it is true statistically that children are most likely to suffer abuse from a trusted family member,[5] it is not always the

5. *Myths and Facts about child sexual abuse.* Rape Crisis Federation Wales and England, see page 14, footnote 1.

case that abuse is due to brokenness in a family. Whilst background and past experiences can be negative and lead people to make wrong or unhelpful decisions, many who have very difficult and broken family backgrounds go on to establish healthy family lifestyles. Sometimes abusers refuse to accept responsibility for what they have done by claiming that their behaviour is a result of coming from a broken family background, but whilst past experiences can to some extent explain why a person behaves in a certain way, they can never be an excuse for abusive behaviour of any sort. Ultimately each human being has to take responsibility for his or her own actions.

In a healthy family, there should be care, consideration and a positive climate of love. Communicating should bring pleasure and fulfilment. Family members should feel accepted and valued, with the freedom to have their own opinions, even when those opinions differ greatly from those of other family members. The family should take part in healthy and enjoyable activities together, which will provide opportunities for personal growth and development.

Every family faces challenges in relating, because no individual or group is perfect. Most families experience times when communication and relating is difficult or even breaks down completely due to stressful circumstances, possibly a death, a serious illness or some other traumatic event. Once a crisis has passed, healthy families tend to return to their normal ways of functioning.

Some families manage to stay together despite severe degrees of brokenness, caused perhaps by bereavement, serious illness or domestic violence. However, ongoing brokenness in families can produce insecurities and be a breeding ground for other problems. In a family that struggles for one reason or another, it may not have taken any particular trauma to provoke the unhealthy roles and behaviour. The problems of such families tend to be long term and complex, and children's needs are not usually met, either emotionally, physically or even materially. Negative patterns of behaviour will probably dominate the child's life, growth and development.

It is widely acknowledged that family life and the effect it has upon a person is fundamental to individual development and growth. Nowadays our concept of what a family is does not necessarily demand both a father and a mother; there can be all kinds of combinations and mixtures of parents, step-parents, single parents. Whether this leads to a confusion of roles and is unhelpful for the child is a matter of debate amongst professionals. What cannot be denied is that father and mother role models are especially important in a child's formative years.

Much research has been done to examine the importance of a baby's relationship with mother and father in the first few years of life. John Bowlby is a psychiatrist who has done research into the effects of separation and loss in small children. He has demonstrated that the attachment of the infant to the mother is of overwhelming importance in determining the individual's later sense of security and success in forming relationships with others, and that separation from or loss of a mother, at a young age, can have a devastating effect.[6] Whatever the reason for the separation, counsellors call this absence of a mother 'separation anxiety'. It is caused by a lack of bonding with the mother, and this bonding process between mother and child is particularly important in the first few years of life. The father also has a significant part to play in a child's welfare, in addition to what the mother offers. Substitute carers can also do an excellent job when the natural parents are not around for the child.

---

6. John Bowlby, author of *Attachment* and also *Separation: Anxiety And Anger*.

Family Games

Psychologists and counsellors in general understand that, to a greater or lesser extent, individuals may play specific roles within families. In broken and troubled families, because the chosen style of relating within such families tends to be negative and not as healthy as in other families, such role-playing can have more damaging consequences. Individuals often adopt these roles in an attempt to prevent any further hurt, either to themselves or to other family members. Examples of the kind of roles people adopt include:

- *The hero or rescuer role.* This is an attempt to solve problems in the short term, whereby the family member tries to act as the one who has all the solutions. He or she feels responsible for rescuing the situation and/or all the people involved. This person will be proactive and always seem to have the right answer to every predicament. Ultimately the problems will still be there, unresolved, and the 'hero' has taken on needless responsibility and may be left with feelings of inadequacy and failure because he or she really believed a solution could be found.

- *The lost child role.* This strategy enables the person to isolate themselves from the real situation by ignoring the circumstances and taking no responsibility for anything. These family members are usually silent and tend not to be noticed by others. This withdrawal into a seemingly safe world isolates them and prevents meaningful relationships.

- *The mascot role.* Adopting this role allows someone to distract other family members by entertaining them, preventing people from facing up to the real issues. Mascots provide comic relief for the family's crisis. The underlying assumption is that the painful issues will resolve themselves without being faced head–on. The mascot can be a lonely, angry person whilst appearing to be someone who is always clowning and having fun.

- *The saint role.* This sort of person is the 'evangelist' or 'priest' in a family, and their self-elected remit is to 'save' everyone from sure disaster. The saint, or prime enabler, is someone who sees it as their task to keep the family together at all costs. Such people look and act as if everything is under their control, but they are motivated by a fear of everything collapsing around them.

- *The surrogate spouse role.* This is someone who becomes the little mummy or daddy in a family where the parents are not fulfilling their proper roles.

- *The scapegoat role.* This is someone who wrongly believes that he or she is the reason for the problem and develops a complex set of defences in an attempt to try to resolve feelings of blame and responsibility. Everything that is wrong is perceived to be entirely his or her fault. The person feels it to be necessary for others to blame the scapegoat, because that will put everything right. The predominant feelings are guilt and shame, both of which have a damaging effect on relationships, because these are blockages to right relating. Guilt and shame will always get in the way of the freedom to relate in a healthy way.

- *The problem person role.* This kind of family member indulges in unhealthy behaviour which contributes significantly to unhealthy family dynamics. An example would be someone who has an obvious life-controlling problem such as alcoholism or drug abuse. Inside, such a person will be full of deprivation.

- *The activist role.* Someone who is always constrained to 'do' something to resolve the situation. This person will be energetic, busy and involved. There can be negative consequences, in that the real roots of problems are never addressed. The 'doing' tends to paper over the issues, which means the unresolved situation continues to worsen.

Not all these roles are necessarily negative or unhelpful all of the time, but assuming any of them can stop an abused person from moving on into healing and freedom. The person who has been the family mascot, for instance, who may be very amusing, is really hiding behind a mask of humour. Defusing an uncomfortable or potentially dangerous situation at the time may not allow issues to come into the open and be addressed. Understanding the roles that they have adopted for themselves over the years will help hurting people to take a step towards resolving those personal issues which have come about through being abused.

The rewards of relating

Whenever I think about relationships, I immediately think of chutney! When I first made chutney its main ingredients seemed surprising, because vinegar and sugar are so totally different. It was hard to imagine using them in the same recipe, let alone plums and onions; yet when put together they are delicious. It's rather like that with relationships. People can relate well to different types of personalities, and sometimes opposites attract. One look at any group of people who enjoy each other's company surely shows that God's ways are not our ways! Sometimes the best friendships or marriages are between people who appear to be the exact opposite of each other.

The rewards of good relationships are endless, and I am convinced that it is part of God's plan that everyone should have healthy friendships with both men and women. The joys of friendship can add greatly to a person's quality of life and sense of purpose.

One girl, whom I will call Sarah, was outraged by her abuser, a member of her family, because he let her take all the blame for his abuse by keeping silent. She was so keen to get everything put behind her that she confessed to being at fault for the abuse, which was not actually possible given her tender years. All this did was push the truth underground and delay her healing. A consequence of this was that Sarah was 'no good at relationships' according to her own thinking, but she was very wrong about this. Underneath all the defences she developed to keep people at bay, she was keen to relate to other people, and particularly to men, whom she had consistently avoided. Sarah did not sit with any of the men at the coffee break at work and she befriended only single girls 'in case there were complications', although this reasoning was largely subconcious. Slowly part of her feelings wakened up to noticing men and wanting to have safe contact. Sarah joined a class connected with a hobby of hers. Initially she appeared to take a great interest in the work in hand, which was a cover for being too scared to speak to the people in the class. Slowly she looked up from her work and began to interact with those around her, both men and women. Although nothing major happened in her circumstances, something major did happen in her heart. At the start of the second term of the class, it was as though an entirely different girl had appeared. Sarah began to think that relating might not be so bad after all. Now that she is more positive about life and relating to people more easily as a result of addressing these issues through counselling, the joy of relating in healthy ways is observable on her face.

Of course, everyone has varying degrees of struggle in relationships because we live in an imperfect world. Reactions to what is said and to events can be variable and unpredictable, whether or not these events are negative or positive. As we go through life, it becomes ever more obvious that not everyone interprets words and actions in the same way. Learning to deal with that and not always interpret a negative or critical response as a personal attack, is an important element in developing and maintaining good relationships, but can be particularly hard for those whose self-esteem and confidence have been damaged.

The damage done through sexual abuse is such that it takes a significant degree of healing in order to relate in a satisfying way. It has to be said, however, that some abused people go ahead and relate closely and appear to have no difficulty. For example, it is fairly often the case that an abused person will attempt to bury emotional pain and go on to have a very successful marriage, being conscious of no particular symptoms. It is also possible to find relating to people just too difficult. In such a case a person may behave rather like a butterfly, dipping in and out of relationships and never allowing closeness.

One man, whom I shall call Percy, was so wounded by childhood abuse that he went on a search for a good relationship, although he had no idea how to relate. Percy was looking to have his own needs met and constantly used people to meet these needs. He developed a lifestyle that involved one-night stands because, underneath it all, he was terrified to relate to women. Prostitutes, who provided a service, did not of course look to him for security, marriage or relationship, so he felt he was on safe ground. Percy came looking for counselling help when he realised that he was in a worse mess because of his lifestyle. He felt that parts of him were left all over the country and that he had effectively got lost. Counselling showed Percy that one of his root issues was looking for his mother's approval, his mother being the one who had abused him. She died in a psychiatric hospital, having been estranged from her entire family. Her health did not allow for any useful dialogue before she died, and Percy had to come to terms with this. It felt like beginning again for Percy to deal with all the childhood issues before trying to relate in the present day. However, this gave him understanding into his behaviour. One insight he got was that there had never been a good feminine role model for him. An older lady, with whom he learned to have an appropriate friendship, met this need. She was a neighbour. In fact, Percy thinks she was the first good female role model he really tried to relate to. Counselling helped him to see how he could have his needs met without using people. This was revolutionary for him. With fantastic courage, Percy persisted in learning to relate. He now has two good friends who are ladies and who, he insists, he treats as ladies. Friendship has turned him around. Percy would tell you that healthy relating is worth aiming for!

Jesus and relationships

Many Christians have found that learning to trust God and go to him for guidance makes a huge difference when trying to build relationships with other people.

When Jesus walked this earth he gave us a model for right relationships, both with his Father and with the many people he encountered. He had close and intimate friends. He also had devoted followers and disciples. There is no record of Jesus ever having to apologise. His relationships were faultless.

One specific example is Jesus' relationship with Lazarus, whose home Jesus used to visit. John's Gospel tells us, 'Jesus loved Martha and her sister and Lazarus' (John 11:5). When he heard of Lazarus' death, Jesus wept. He fully involved himself in the grief and mourning, even though he knew that Lazarus would rise from the dead. 'When Mary reached the place where

Jesus was and saw him, she fell at his feet and said, "Lord, if you had been here, my brother would not have died." When Jesus saw her weeping, and the Jews who had come along with her also weeping, he was deeply moved in spirit and troubled. "Where have you laid him?" he asked. "Come and see, Lord", they replied. Jesus wept. Then the Jews said, "See how he loved him!"' (John 11:32-36).

Just as he felt with and for his friends, we can be confident that Jesus fully involves himself in the grief and mourning that comes from abuse because of his heart of love for all mankind. If we were able to apply in our own lives some of Jesus' teachings and his example, there would be far fewer relationship problems. It is wonderful that Jesus was able to relate to both Martha and Mary, two sisters who were quite different people. He also had meaningful and good relationships with twelve disciples, who must have thrown up a fair number of issues between them! He dealt with unsatisfactory situations in the local church (John 2:12-16) and even took on church leaders when they needed to adjust their thinking (Matt. 15:1-9)!

Jesus defended a lady who was caught in an adulterous situation and suggested to those who judged her that he who was guiltless should throw the first stone. Jesus knew men's hearts and they all retreated without stoning the lady (John 8:1-11). This transformed the woman and she had a different life afterwards.

Jesus has also transformed Heather, as she tells us:

Coming to know Jesus and relate to him has transformed my relationships altogether. No stone has been left unturned, as the love of God has shown me how to relate to my self, to God and to other people. His school of learning is a tough one, because lots of my thinking had to be turned upside down. I was concerned that I would never be able to crack this relationship thing but with perseverance I will get there. Church has become more helpful lately now that they have got used to the more honest me. It wasn't that I was dishonest before, but I know myself better now. My walk with God has been exciting and has been the foundation for mending my other relationships.

CHAPTER 7

DAMAGED SEXUALITY

Where there has been a lack of good role models in child-hood, or some family brokenness that has not helped to form a wholesome view of sexuality, insecurities can appear in regard to gender and sexual identity. A child's understanding of gender roles and sexuality is influenced by a number of factors, including home background and parental views and experience. Sexually abusive experience will very probably have a distorting and confusing effect on a child's development in this area, which may lead to sexual issues becoming a source of difficulty in later life.

Maleness and femaleness
The Bible says that God created people as male or female (Gen. 1:27). However, there is a lot of confusion in today's world about gender issues. 'Sex' tends to be used almost exclusively for the biological act of sexual intercourse. 'Gender' is used to describe the differences between men and women, and this includes generally held perceptions about the way men and women most often react or behave, which may vary to some extent from one culture to another. For example, the power to

initiate, analytical reasoning and proactive problem solving are generally regarded as being qualities found more often in men than women, and so will be counted as 'masculine' qualities. Using the same criteria, examples of feminine qualities include responsiveness, nurturing and intuition. Most people will have a combination of so-called 'masculine' and 'feminine' qualities, whatever their biological sex.

In a child's formative years, it is his or her father and mother, or other people who provide significant role models, who communicate the concept of what maleness and femaleness actually is.

Confused sexuality

One of the most profound and damaging effects of abuse is the confusion it can cause in relation to gender. This is not surprising, since sexual abuse involves a violation of the most private physical, sexual and emotional aspects of a person's life.

There can be an imbalance or separation of the masculine and feminine qualities within a person. For example, in order to protect herself from further harm, a woman may tend to embrace more masculine qualities, by understating her femininity in how she dresses. In other words, she cuts herself off from her femininity as a defence mechanism. I remember one such lady, who shaved the hair off her head every morning, wore no jewellery or make-up, and walked like a man. She was completely denying her sexuality because of her father's dislike of her femininity. He rejected her at birth and went on to sexually abuse her until she was an adult. She developed a severe hatred of all feminine attributes to please her father. Such confusion can obviously cause difficulties in relating to the opposite sex, and may therefore stop the normal, healthy development of relationships. It may also lead to other, less obviously linked problems, such as envy of those who are able to relate successfully.

Any sexual contact or experience that is imposed on and against a person's will or volition may cause trauma and confusion about both gender and sexuality. One of the issues when actually being abused is the confrontation of another's sexuality with one's own sexuality in a negative and harmful way. As a result, relationships with those of the same sex as the abuser can be shunned, or embraced in a negative way. Fear of experiencing one's own sexuality after abuse can prevent relationship growth. People who have been abused may feel safer with large protective barriers around their body, emotions and sexuality, and even around any expression of that sexuality. Countless people have gone into great detail with me about how it is safer to appear to be sexually neutral, which involves denying their sexuality through the image they portray. Things such as the way people dress, their make-up, jewellery and hairstyle, all affect the image they project to the world around them. Consciously or subconsciously everyone makes choices in these areas, which in turn reflect how comfortable a person is with his or her sexual identity. This is one of the areas deep within a person's being which can be much affected by abuse, but it is quite possible to be unaware that abuse has influenced issues such as, for instance, what is worn or how hair is styled.

In counselling, I have met men who, as a direct result of having been being abused, never want to consider marriage. For these men, relating to women has become too uncomfortable or intimidating. Henry found that his attempts at relating, especially to women, were often very unhappy episodes:

> I was left sexually confused by my two abusers and as a result turned to relating to the same sex. Attempts at this were catastrophic and actually confused me further. There was a need for contact, a need for connection, and I found women altogether too scary. Perhaps I was replicating the pain of the abuse in trying to diminish it. This was entirely in vain. The

whole effect was to make relating more tense and strained than it was before. I knew I wasn't gay, but I could have continued down that road had the grace of God not stopped me. I made some major wrong choices in terms of my sexual identity and relationships, not understanding until much later that these choices were rooted in my response to the abuse I had suffered. Confusion and disorientation reigned for years.

Further down the line I dared to dip my toes into a potential relationship with a woman. Although I was attracted to her, my fear reached fever pitch. The way I eventually found healing was by realising that I had some unhelpful and wrong beliefs about sexuality and relating. These were corrected one by one, as I was able to look at them. Sometimes I got help by talking to friends. I also found it useful on a daily basis to stop all self-hatred and confusion by agreeing in my own mind on some positive statements and rehearsing them instead of all the accustomed negativity. For example, 'no woman will ever look twice at me', became, 'I am a good-looking man and attractive to women'. This took a bit of doing, but reaped great rewards over time.[1]

I also remember one client, whom I shall call Carol, who repeatedly chose unhealthy relationships and each time received considerable hurt. It took quite a bit of effort on her part to see that she was setting herself up for disaster because of her negative view of her sexuality and generally low opinion of herself. When she learned to respect herself and have appropriate boundaries in place, she easily conveyed the message that her relationships were going to be far more positive and healthy. Carol later married and experienced joy both in her relating and in the experience of sexuality within a right and positive environment.

---

1. For further reading see Leanne Payne, *Crisis in Masculinity*, Kingsway, Sussex, 1985.

Heather too has experienced difficulties in this area of sexuality:

I had no idea that denial of my femininity was so deeply embedded within me. I would observe other women and know that I was different. Trying to pin it down wasn't at all easy. Basically I wasn't comfortable inside my own body. My non-verbal communication was clearly defensive. I wanted all men to stay away from me. In essence I didn't want to present as attractive in case I was abused or sexually propositioned. In reality I never thought that I was attractive. Every man was a threat to me, whether young or old. This is why I felt a little safer with my friends' husbands rather than single men. Surely, I thought, they wouldn't look twice at me.

I covered up my femininity with baggy clothes. Make-up and jewellery were a waste of money according to me. I sometimes felt happier if I put on weight – I thought to myself that that would reduce my chances of a sexual attack. It didn't – a perfect stranger in a public place attacked me! My reaction was so extreme that it gave one of my friends a clue that there must be some other hurt deep down inside me that was suppressed. The conscious knowledge of being abused lay dormant for another ten to fifteen years after that sexual attack.

I found it difficult to even walk in front of others or be seen by them. Everything in me wanted to hide from being a woman, and I worked very hard to protect myself. At the same time I did 'notice' men, and wondered if there was one somewhere who was non-abusive. I had labelled all men as being the same. I now know that I was wrong and am thrilled to say that through lots of hard work and God-given patient friends, I am being healed – enough to say it is good to be a woman! It is the Lord who has done this work of healing within me.

Since women tend to be more emotional and less visually driven in their sexuality, whilst men are more visual and less emotional, they tend to express sexual brokenness in contrasting ways. For example, sexual addiction is more common amongst men; conversely, emotional dependency is more common amongst women. So, for instance, addiction to internet pornography is much more prevalent amongst men, whilst women may retreat into a fantasy world, often fuelled by romantic novels. The emotional response to sexual abuse in women can lead to frigidity, a shunning of any sexual contact. On the other hand, both men and women can experience an insatiable sexual appetite or an unspoken pursuit of sexual contact without relationship as a direct result of having been abused. Often this is a subconscious drive to seek out further pain, in an attempt to cover the inner pain that already exists. Flora comments, 'Where a pattern of abuse has been established, there is comfort in completing that pattern through even more abuse. And once the worst has happened, one can stop dreading it.'

To be unwillingly aroused before or during puberty, through being raped or abused for example, can bring a sexual awareness long before it would normally be appropriate, and may be accompanied by, for instance, nightmares or self-harm. Even young children can be prematurely sexualised through abuse and by being primed for abuse. This may lead to masturbation or an apparent desire for more illicit sexual contact. The end result is more sexual confusion, more hurt and more emotional pain.

Causes of abuse

Many abused people feel that it was something about them as an individual that prompted their abuser to single them out, but it needs to be understood that even if that were true it does not mean they were to blame and could never justify an abuser's actions. Since most sexual abuse happens within the family home and is carried out by someone known to and trusted by the abused person, opportunity, circumstances and chance are the more probable explanations as to why abuse happens to a particular individual.

There can be many underlying causes that lead people to sexually abuse others. These may include an experience of having been abused themselves, family problems in the past, low self-esteem, insecurities or an inability to form satisfying relationships for a variety of reasons. This does not excuse abusers or diminish their responsibility, but it can give some insight into why they behave in this unacceptable way. The very nature of abuse indicates that it is not usually a momentary lapse of morality. There may have been years of accumulated secrets, manipulation and deception, leading to someone going on to abuse over a sustained period of time.

Another catalyst to abusive behaviour can be exposure to pornography, either in magazines, on TV or the Internet. In the last few years I have noticed a marked increase in men coming for counselling help because of an addiction to internet pornography. I firmly believe that pornography can be the thin end of the wedge that leads people to commit abusive acts, and its ready availability in our society is deeply worrying, especially in light of its potentially damaging effect on impressionable pubescent boys. As one Christian commentator on abuse has said:

> The proliferation of pornography accessible to everyone, adults and children alike, is becoming astonishingly open and available. Our society is becoming immune to what only twenty years ago was considered unfit by even worldly standards. Pornography seems to fill a deep crack in the heart that never got mended in holy ways. It brings a temporary titillation and comfort to the surface of the problems of the

soul rather than providing the deep total healing of the roots of neediness.[2]

It should also be recognised that the actual production of pornographic material is itself abusive of those photographed. As I have been writing this book, I have been sickened yet again at a news report of a paedophile ring that the police have uncovered in London. Apparently they found a mountain of pornographic images, and photographs of at least 52 haunted–looking children, whom they are now trying to trace. That should be sufficient proof that pornography is harmful, whether or not it leads those who 'enjoy' it into abusive activities.

More about power than sex

A major contributory factor in sexual abuse is accessibility to the child, elderly or disabled person, or whoever is chosen for abuse. Child abuse, for example, often occurs when a person older or stronger than the child uses his or her power, authority or position of trust to involve a child in sexual behaviour or activity. An abuser will often use manipulation, deceit and control in an attempt to distort a person's judgment. The idea is to keep access to the person they can abuse by leading them to believe that what is happening is perfectly acceptable. There may be an attempt to blackmail the abused person into believing there is no way that the abuse can be stopped.[3] Abusive relationships always involve an element of control, whereby the abuser controls the abused person in negative ways in an attempt to continue the abuse secretly. There may also be a false

---

2. Signa Bodisbaugh, 'The Christian's battle with Pornography' in *The Journey to Wholeness in Christ Newsletter*, Christ Episcopal Church, Mobile, Alabama, 1998. Signa Bodisbaugh has a new book, *Illusions of Intimacy*, Sovereign World, Kent, 2004.
3. See *Games abusers play* in chapter 1.

sense of loyalty to the abuser, who makes the person feel they are obligated to allow continuing abuse or to keep quiet about the abuse, even though this is clearly against the conscious wishes of the person being abused. In most cases the abused person reports having felt overpowered, but admitting this takes courage, as it is a seeming admission of personal weakness.

An abused person often asks the question, 'Why did he or she abuse me?' Studies show that the motive for sexual abuse is not primarily sexual pleasure or satisfaction, but has more to do with power, control, domination and humiliation.[4] There is always a power imbalance in abusive relationships. Abusers have told us about the inner anger and violence that motivated them to indulge in abusive behaviour. This anger can be rooted in their own deep hurts and unresolved issues from the past. One abuser told us that after being released from prison, it was Christian counselling that helped him to see that abusing his grandchild was his way of using 'sex' as a weapon against his ex-wife and daughter. Since he could not touch either of them, he took out his wrath on his grandchild. He was unconscious of his motive for abusing until he explored all the roots of his own problems and insecurities.

If sexual abuse is a means of power and control, it is hardly surprising that one encounters cases where brothers and sisters abuse their siblings, fathers their children, mothers their children, schoolteachers and doctors those they are professionally responsible for.

Abusers need help

Abusers usually need specialist help and intervention appropriate to their needs if they are to change and cease to be a

---

4. For instance, see study by the Rape Crisis Federation Wales and England, page 14, footnote 1.

danger to others. It is not sufficient for an abuser to say 'sorry' and then to expect everything to be forgiven and forgotten. The roots of why the abuse happened have to be explored and insights gained in order to bring about change in the person and to prevent any further occurrence of abuse in the future. The danger of someone reoffending is something that has to be taken very seriously, and a former abuser needs to be closely monitored. Specialist help might include specific and expert counselling, a period in specialist residential care, therapy in prison, ongoing accountability, supported housing. and psychiatric or psychological help.

It is essential that the abuser take responsibility for all he or she has done against people and against God if he (or she) is to change his behaviour and refrain from any future involvement in abusing people. Much counsel and prayer is needed, with supported accountability regarding behaviour and future responsibilities. This includes the breaking of established bad habits and patterns. An abuser needs to seek help in order to start on the road to recovery. There is hope, and help is available.[5]

In prison, many sexual offenders require protection, because other prisoners feel a disgust at the sexual acts they have committed against vulnerable people, especially children. In society at large, sexual offenders are frequently shunned, and people generally don't want to have them living in their neighbourhood. Understandably, fear motivates parents to want to protect their children if they discover that a sex offender is living in their locality. These may be understandable reactions,

---

5. Help is available from Broken Yoke Ministries, Bob Domelen, PO Box 361, Waukesha, W153187-0361, USA, email RobertVBY@juno.com, www.brokenyoke.org. Dove Christian Counselling work with abusers who are prepared to look at the roots of their difficulties. Dove Christian Counselling, 110 St. James Road, Glasgow, G4 0PS. Tel. 0141 552 5120, info@dove.uk.net. For international contact details see the appendix.

but if offenders are to be reintegrated into society, it is vital that there is better understanding of how their behaviour and attitudes can be changed over time so that they present less of a risk to society.

Sexual wholeness

Being content in one's own sexuality is a crucial part of finding healing. God has a perfect plan for human sexuality and healthy expressions of it within his parameters. Society today has moved far from God's plan for sexual relating. It seems that anything is acceptable, creating a climate of confusion and hurt. The joy of sexual fulfilment in a right relationship was God's idea and a good one at that! Our sexuality should be expressed in a secure, loving and monogamous relationship. 'For this reason a man will leave his father and mother and be united to his wife, and they will become one flesh' (Gen. 2:24). God's best is celibacy before marriage. Marriage was God's idea for building a quality relationship between one man and one woman and for providing a stable environment for bringing children into the world.[6]

In the case of rape, where a person is robbed of her (or his) virginity, this is entirely the abuser's fault in God's sight. It is possible to be healed, both emotionally and spiritually, so that this does not become a stumbling–block to a right sexual relationship or to raising a child conceived through rape.[7]

It has been a great joy to work with some very brave people who have faced all their personal and sexual issues and have

---

6. See 1 Corinthians 7.
7. It may be helpful to look at blame and guilt in chapter 3. AMICA is a Pregnancy Crisis Centre, 29 Nicolson Square, (above Clydesdale Bank), Edinburgh, EH8 9BX, Tel. 0131 667 7800, enquiries@amicapcc.org. For international contact details see appendix.

come through to healing. One such person is Joyce, who was a sad soul when she first came for counselling. Her life was a mess, with a catalogue of torn relationships and painful emotions. Joyce seemed keen to relate to men, but backed off as soon as anyone looked for a commitment. After getting some help, Joyce began to understand that her plan in relating to men was to make them suffer and to take out how she felt about her abuser on any man that got close to her. With great courage Joyce faced the roots of her behaviour, and over time managed to deal with bitterness, anger and a serious mistrust of the opposite sex. Now she is able to relate more healthily with men both at work and socially. She feels that although she has never had the opportunity to be married, she has discovered contentment in her life as a single person. It has been a delight to watch Joyce face her issues and come to a place of peace about being a woman.

Another client, called Alan, had no memory of ever being sexually abused until his wedding night. All of a sudden he remembered that he had suffered at the hands of an older woman. This had not been in his conscious mind at all, and came as a tremendous shock to both him and his new wife. The trouble was that he saw his abuser's face instead of his wife's in intimate situations, and this was intolerable for him. His immediate response was to feel an utter failure as a husband and to want to run away from his wife. Thankfully he sought immediate help from his doctor, who suggested he get counselling as soon as possible. What we did with Alan was to help him face his personal pain and hurt emotions before working with them as a couple, although we did see his wife once in the early stages so that she understood the process.

As Alan told us his story of abuse, it sounded as if this was the first time he had said it even to himself. To cope, he had buried what had happened, but he had also earnestly believed that abuse only happened to girls. Once he named his abuse for what it was, he began to want to blame his abuser and he needed to think back over his past and see it as it really was. Always a shy man, scared around the opposite sex, Alan began to see the root of his fear. He remembered that he thought it was amazing that his wife wanted to marry him and that she loved him. This was because his self-esteem was non-existent.

There is a marvellous sequel to Alan's story. As he faced his pain, blamed his abuser and took a variety of steps to make peace with his past, he became the best husband ever – so his wife said! Initially she had been horrified that intimacy turned her new husband into an anxious and traumatised character whom she didn't recognise. At first she thought it must be her fault, but after a few days, when Alan was clearly distressed, he shared his story with her. Although she knew nothing about abuse, she did know she wanted this new husband of hers to get help, and supported him throughout the process. The doctor advised against intimacy for a while since it was so distressing, but encouraged Alan and his wife to have hope that this could all be mended. It would take a bit of time, he told them, and he was right. It was fully six months before Alan stopped 'seeing' his abuser's face. The trauma of all that happened has strengthened this marriage, and both would say that they are glad such a positive thing as a good marriage could bring this abuse to light so that it could be sorted out at the very core of Alan's being.

Whilst Alan's story had a happy ending, he is still working on layers of healing in his life and in his marriage. However, his story illustrates a number of elements that are common to finding sexual wholeness:

- He sought appropriate help, despite his great embarrassment.
- He got support from those who loved him.

- He told no one except those he had to.
- He knew it would take a period of time before he could expect to be healed.
- He faced the past layer by layer as he felt able.
- He bravely learned to see that his wife was not his abuser. The sexual distortions were faced and altered as he committed to making right choices (in Alan's case he had to establish in his thinking and with his feelings that he had not married his abuser and that his wife loved him and did not want to hurt him). In other words, Alan committed to believing the truth despite how he felt.
- The power of the abuser was challenged and broken as issues were dealt with.
- As a Christian, he and his wife prayed together as they faced this unexpected trauma. Knowing God was with them helped their faith to grow and to get through difficult days.

Putting these principles into practice has helped many to move beyond their brokenness. I hope the stories in this chapter convey the fact there really is hope for both the abused and abusers.

EPILOGUE

LIVES RENEWED

This chapter was written in spring when new growth and signs of new life bring renewed hope. Easter is a time when Christians remember the life, death and resurrection of Jesus Christ. This brings much hope for life now and in eternity. Abused people, male or female, young or old, rich or poor need hope for healing: hope for today and for the future. This is God's promise: "'For I know the plans I have for you," declares the Lord, "plans to prosper you and not to harm you, plans to give you hope and a future'" (Jer. 29:11).

One lady who is living in the light of this promise today is someone who has appeared several times in this book, and whom I have called Flora. Her sad story is not untypical, in my experience, but she has found hope in the midst of her search for healing:

> When I was thirty-six, my daughter turned six, and all hell broke loose in my life. Until that moment I had managed to hold together a façade of triumphalistic Christianity. I sang in the worship group at my church, led a women's Bible study group, and taught in the Sunday School. I was a 'good Christian wife', although it was becoming increasingly difficult to maintain the active sex life recommended by St Paul. As I had

small children to care for, I'd been able to gloss over my inability to go out to work, since I could be a 'good Christian mother' by staying at home. Now, suddenly, I could no longer cope.

I always knew I had been abused by our lodger when I was eight. The much more violent assault I had suffered from another predator when I was six had been completely blocked out, until my daughter's fateful birthday began the process of bringing it and other memories to the surface.

My life since then has been a kind of pilgrimage, based around Christ's words, 'You shall know the truth, and the truth will set you free'. I haven't arrived yet, and the roads I have travelled have been long and dark, but with bursts of light so glorious that they dazzle. I'm not nearly such a 'good' Christian as I used to be, but I'm a much more real person, and I live in a world where beauty moves the heart, food has a taste, and broken people carry one another's burdens. I think God's face lights up when he looks my way.

I know of no sexually abused person who chose to be abused. Sometimes it can be fearful to imagine what may be involved in getting well. Abuse has a binding, crippling effect and facing the legacy of torn emotions takes huge courage. However, many clients have expressed the view that dealing with the issues and symptoms have made them stronger people. Healing is not about the absence of pain. Healing is much more about moving into the depths of new life stage by stage: more to do with pain fitting into someone's life than allowing it to remain obstructive and controlling.

On this theme Heather and Henry want the last word!

Henry says:

Career-wise I excelled, rising to the top of my profession, but inside I was in turmoil. I was abused by two men, hurt by two girlfriends, and retreated into myself at a fast rate of knots. Church was significant for me. Friendship was available and lots of social contact, but for a considerable time my deep yearning for healing went unheeded. I could not voice my inner turmoil. Emotionally I was so cut off from myself, that, looking back, the years seem empty. Lost years really, with a defensive desire not to be hurt again which excluded the possibility of quality relationships with either sex.

The healing I have had has been astonishing. The difference it has made has given me peace and joy and wholeness that I never thought was possible this side of Heaven. Each new day is now a gift from God, not something heavy and stressful. God has lovingly challenged many of my diseased attitudes, wrong beliefs and tendencies towards introspection. I am far less egocentric, am now sure of my identity in Christ Jesus, have taken the abuse to the Lord and he has, layer by layer, been healing me significantly over seventeen years. Often I used to wonder if I would ever get to the end of my symptoms and my internal woes. God encouraged me from Exodus 23:29-30: 'But I will not drive them out in a single year, because the land would become desolate and the wild animals too numerous for you. Little by little I will drive them out before you, until you have increased enough to take possession of the land.'

It has been a privilege to share with the readers of this book about my life. Thinking back I am amazed at the route my life has taken. I feel my abuse is in the past, although occasionally something will come to mind or I will feel sad. What I would really like to say to the readers of this book is that life is good and the road to healing is worth pursuing despite the inevitable ups and downs. I don't see that what I have done is courageous. What I had to face I had to face and other people have other things to face. Each person has his or her own challenges. I am a stronger person now that I have learned to say 'no' and to operate within what is comfortable for me. My wife and I are truly happy and she has been very long-suffering and patient.

Heather comments:

> As this book has unfolded, my own journey towards healing
> has continued. I honestly don't know what kind of person I
> would have been if my daddy had not abused me. It is part
> of my life and has been the biggest reason that made me seek
> help and, in the long run, to pursue a better quality of life.
> My anger has gone and I have forgiven my daddy and all the
> circumstances surrounding my abuse. Relationships might
> have been less complex if I had not been abused, or maybe I
> am kidding myself. Friends have been so kind and caring and
> have shown me real love. The people I have met, especially
> those who took time to listen to my heart, have enriched my
> life. I am pretty sure I have grown spiritually because of my
> past. God has always been there for me. Sometimes I meet
> other people who have been abused and I'd like to think I have
> been able to draw alongside and encourage them.

In conclusion I would like to share a story of healing that may
bring hope to the hurting. It is in the form of a vision, and was
passed on to me by a close friend, who felt that it expressed
what it is like to be freed from the painful effects of abuse:

> Unveiled before me was a scene of children playing in a court-
> yard. When two women entered the picture I realised what
> was strange about the whole scenario. All but these two wom-
> en were hobbling and limping, even the small children. One
> of these women lifted a child and sat her on a low wall and
> as she did so I was drawn to something strange on the child's
> feet. The women asked the child why her feet were so tightly
> bound and I heard the child say that it was the tradition to do
> this to girls' feet from infancy. These little ones had no power
> to object or break free and consequently their feet became de-
> formed and they were never able to walk unhindered.
>   One of the ladies gently cradled two tiny feet in her lap and
> slowly began to unwind the crushing black bands that bound

the tiny feet. The trembling child began to struggle and cry out in fear and pain. The girl's anguish and pain-wracked cries were sandwiched between growing sighs of relief. I watched, my breath catching in my throat, as the tears that fell from the cheeks of the lady kissed those tiny, bruised and crushed feet. This precious child had to go through pain in order to experience freedom from what had bound her for years. It was her only hope of walking properly. Then she would grow and flourish. I saw the two ladies pick up the girl in their arms. They carried her to a quiet spot and applied ointment and massaged those tiny feet, and I saw them help the child take her first step. She walked, gingerly holding on to them for support. Later she simply held an arm, and eventually walked alongside them, unaided.

The little girl was not only free but she was supported and drawn by the tears and hands of love held out to her as she made her first faltering steps. So it is for each person as faltering steps are taken into life beyond abuse. God reaches down and takes hold of the person with never–ending love and compassion. He has a tailor-made healing programme to suit every individual. He gathers all the tears of pain and with compassion and love turns them into pure drops of gold.

APPENDIX

International resources
A number of agencies and helpful resources are mentioned throughout this book. The following is a list of similar agencies in other countries. The author, having no personal knowledge of the organisations, has been unable to evaluate them and caution is recommended in using their services.

United States of America
www.gospelcom.net/guidance
Online Guidance
This site includes biblical guidance on such topics as alcohol abuse, divorce, and grief.

www.salvationarmyusa.org
Salvation Army
Tel. 703 684 5500

www.newlife.com
Includes information on a wide variety of counselling topics.

www.walking-wounded.net
Sexual abuse (Christian)

www.alcoholicsforchrist.com
Tel. 1 800 441 7877 (US and Canada)
Email: al4christ@globalbiz.net

www.christians-in-recovery.org/db
Christian Recovery Resources Database, listing 2,000 Local
Christian Support Groups. Organisations, Programs, Group
Meetings and Counsellors in the US & Canada and outside of
North America.

www.remudaranch.com
Christian Eating Disorders

www.fmsfonline.org
The False Memory Syndrome Foundation
Address: 1955 Locust Street, Philadelphia, PA 19103-5766
Tel. 215 940 1040, Fax 215-940-1042.
Email: mail@fmsfonline.org

www.survivors-and-friends.org
Survivors and Friends exists to provide hope, encouragement,
and support for survivors of sexual abuse, their friends, and
their family.

www.nmha.org
National Mental Health Association
Tel. 1 800 931 2237

Hotlines in United States of America
National Youth Crisis Hotline Tel. 1 800 448 4663
Provides counselling and referrals to local drug treatment
centres, shelters, and counselling services. Responds to youth
dealing with pregnancy, molestation, suicide, and child abuse.

Rape & Abuse & Incest National Network Tel. 1 800 656-HOPE

National Child Abuse Hotline Tel. 1-800-4-A-CHILD
(TDD) Tel. 1-800-2-A-CHILD
Provides multilingual crisis intervention and professional counselling on child abuse. Gives referrals to local social service groups offering counselling on child abuse. Has literature on child abuse in English and Spanish. Operates 24 hours.
(reaches Canada, Guam, Puerto Rico and the U.S. Virgin Islands)

Eating Disorder Hotline Tel. 1 800 931 2237

Grief Recovery Helpline Tel. 1 800 4454808

National Suicide Hotline Tel. 1 888 248 2587

Canada
Child Abuse Hotline Tel. 1 800 387 KIDS (5437)

Australia
Child Abuse Prevention Services Tel. 1 800 688 009

Advocate for Survivors of Child Abuse Tel. 1 300 657 80

Anorexia and Bulimia Nervosa Association Inc. Tel. 08 8212 1644

South Africa
Childline Tel. 08000 55555

Eating Disorder Unit Tel. 011 489 1206

Christian Focus Publications

publishes books for all ages

Our mission statement –

STAYING FAITHFUL

In dependence upon God we seek to impact the world through literature faithful to his infallible word, the Bible. Our aim is to ensure that the LORD Jesus Christ is presented as the only hope to obtain forgiveness of sin, live a useful life and look forward to heaven with Him.

REACHING OUT

Christ's last command requires us to reach out to our world with His gospel. We seek to help fulfill that by publishing books that point people towards Jesus and help them develop a Christ-like maturity. We aim to equip all levels of readers for life, work, ministry and mission.

Books in our adult range are published in three imprints.

Christian Focus contains popular works including biographies, commentaries, basic doctrine and Christian living. Our children's books are also published in this imprint.

Mentor focuses on books written at a level suitable for Bible College and seminary students, pastors, and other serious readers. The imprint includes commentaries, doctrinal studies, examination of current issues and church history.

Christian Heritage contains classic writings from the past.

Christian Focus Publications Ltd.,
Geanies House, Fearn, Tain
Ross-shire, IV20 1TW, Scotland, United Kingdom
info@christianfocus.com
www.christianfocus.com